PENGUIN PASSNOTES

The Prologue to the Canterbury Tale.

Dr Stephen Coote was educated at Magdalene College, Cambridge, where he was an exhibitioner, and at Birkbeck College, University of London, where he was Sir William Bull Memorial Scholar. He has been an O level examiner and Principal of tutorial colleges in London and Oxford. He has also written a number of books for Penguins and is the Advisory Editor of the Passnotes Series.

PENGUIN PASSNOTES

GEOFFREY CHAUCER

The Prologue to the Canterbury Tales

STEPHEN COOTE M.A., PH.D.

PENGUIN BOOKS

Penguin Books Ltd, Harmondsworth, Middlesex, England
Viking Penguin Inc., 40 West 23rd Street, New York, New York 10010, U.S.A.
Penguin Books Australia Ltd, Ringwood, Victoria, Australia
Penguin Books Canada Limited, 2801 John Street, Markham, Ontario, Canada L3R 1B4
Penguin Books (N.Z.) Ltd, 182–190 Wairau Road, Auckland 10, New Zealand

First published 1985
Reprinted 1986

Made and printed in Great Britain by
Richard Clay (The Chaucer Press) Ltd, Bungay, Suffolk
Filmset in 10/12pt Ehrhardt

*The publishers are grateful to the following Examination Boards for
permission to reproduce questions from examination papers used in
individual titles in the Passnotes series:*

*Associated Examining board, University of Cambridge Local Examinations
Syndicate, Joint Matriculation Board, University of London School
Examinations Department, Oxford and Cambridge Schools Examination
Board, University of Oxford Delegacy of Local Examinations.*

*The Examination Board accept no responsibility whatsoever for the
accuracy or method of working in any suggested answers given as models.*

The copy used for this edition is that of the second edition of
The Complete Works of Geoffrey Chaucer, edited by Rev. W. W. Skeat.
published by Oxford at the Clarendon Press.
with emendations made by the present author.

Contents

Introduction

CHAUCER'S POEM, HIS LIFE AND TIMES

Chaucer's *General Prologue* to the *Canterbury Tales* is one of the most lively descriptions of a group of people ever written, but a first encounter with it may be bewildering in a number of ways. To begin with, the language is tantalizingly remote from our own. As we look at the text, we may recognize a word here, a phrase there and sometimes a full sentence, but many other matters are foreign to us. What, we may ask, is an 'anlas and a gipser al of silk', a 'habergeoun' or a 'vernicle'? Furthermore, though we probably have some general idea of what a pilgrimage is, the vocations of many of the pilgrims themselves are completely strange. We feel confident we know what a priest and a cook might do, but monks are a rare sight and pardoners and summoners utterly unknown.

The reason for this is that Chaucer's poem is nearly six hundred years old and, to appreciate it properly, we have to think ourselves back to a world very different from our own. The confusion we feel is comparable to that which Chaucer himself might experience if we were trying to explain to him the ways of our time. For example, the language we speak is wholly different in pronunciation from Chaucer's. Our language is obviously full of words for objects which Chaucer could never have imagined. We take it for granted that we can talk to people on the other side of the world by telephone, television is a part of our everyday lives, and to none of us is there anything strange about a book like this one, printed on paper and existing in thousands of identical copies.

The books Chaucer would have known, however – the twenty or so that the Clerk is shown as having at the head of his bed, for example – were rare and expensive. All of them were written out by hand on parchment and only a very small number of people could read them.

Most, if they came in contact with a book at all, would usually have it read to them. There is a very beautiful picture in a manuscript of one of Chaucer's poems showing him reading aloud to his audience. This was perfectly normal. And for us, too, it is one of the best ways of becoming familiar with Chaucer. Just as his own audience would have sat and listened to him reading, so we, hearing his lines read out in class or on a record, can become familiar with the proper way in which to pronounce his words and hear the rhythms of his poetry as his audience would have done.

The illustration of Chaucer reading aloud shows that the audience he expected for his work was an aristocratic one: rich, leisured and highly sophisticated. They were, by and large, the descendants of those who had come across to England with William the Conqueror and – quite naturally – they spoke French. Since they were the rulers of the country, French obviously became the medium of government and the law. It was also the language of culture. However, just as we are several hundred years distant from Chaucer, so he and his audience were three and a half centuries removed from the Norman Conquest. England still had many French possessions but she was now a nation in her own right. As such, her own language was developing out of the French of the Normans, the Latin of the Church, and the Anglo-Saxon tongue spoken by the people the Normans had conquered. English was growing up. It was not yet the mature language we speak today. Its grammar was different, its spelling was not fixed, and it contained many words that have now dropped out of usage. All of this presents formidable problems to someone trying to read Chaucer for the first time. A number of suggestions on how to tackle his work have been included (see pp. 13–16), but there is really no substitute for being with a teacher and hearing the poem read aloud. The prose translation included here (see pp. 43–131) may be of some help in clarifying what Chaucer is writing about, but – just as with learning any language – it is essential to hear Chaucer's English spoken, to become familiar with the forms of its grammar and to learn its vocabulary (including particularly those words which – like 'parfit' – have a rather more specialized meaning than at first appears). The notes and glossary will draw your attention to some of these.

We have seen that Chaucer's French-speaking audience was made up largely of aristocrats. This brings us to something else which, like the English they spoke alongside their French, is strange to us: the way that medieval society was structured.

By far the greatest number of the population in Chaucer's England were poor, illiterate and bound to the soil. Their lives and labour were owned by those whose land they worked. To be sure, this feudal structure of society was breaking up, but it was still assumed that the natural order of life was one in which the King appointed by God was at the head and below him were the nobles (like the Knight) who owed him duty. These men had, in their turn, servants and apprentices like the Yeoman and the Squire. The nobility held their lands from the King but they might lease them out or sell them to wealthy members of the middle classes such as the Franklin (literally a 'free man', one not bound to feudal service) or prospering professionals like the Sergeant of the Law. Below these men were humble farmers such as the Ploughman and, below him still, the landless peasantry.

With the growth of business and city life came the growth of the middle classes. Some of these – such as the Sergeant of the Law and the Franklin – Chaucer presents with considerable respect. Others, like the Merchant and the five Guildsmen, he is less generous to. As is usually the case with him, the men of this class whom Chaucer does admire are those with notable professional skills and an optimistic, outgoing attitude to life.

The Church and its influence is a further barrier to our easy familiarity with Chaucer's world. While the hierarchy of Archbishop and Bishop descending down to the humble parish priest may not be wholly unknown, the sheer weight of the Church's presence in Chaucer's England, its variety and the range of ways in which it touched everyday life, is far greater than the presence of the Church today.

The medieval church meant Roman Catholicism. The head of the Catholic church was (and, of course, remains) the Pope. Here was a vast, international organization spreading outwards from Rome to the tiniest and most remote villages. Its language was Latin and its power extensive. Its forms were many. The idea of the humble parish priest is easy enough to grasp, but many other areas of religious life we do not often come across today. Monasticism, for example, is nowhere near as common as it was in Chaucer's time. Again, the begging orders of Friars are something we are unfamiliar with. In medieval England these were commonplace and knowledge of their abuses was wide-spread. The portraits Chaucer offers us of the Monk and the Friar are at the same time individual and representative of whole groups of men whom today we may not easily recognize.

Of all the people attached to the Church, those most unfamiliar today are, without doubt, the Summoner and the Pardoner. The Catholic Church in the Middle Ages had its own laws and courts. The officers who brought men to them were called Summoners. Pardoners, as we shall see, sold forgiveness for cash. Chaucer presents both these characters as dangerously corrupt, and corruption does seem to have been widespread in the Church of his day. Churchmen in the highest and the lowest positions were, as many men knew, often led astray by worldliness and temptation. There was much in the Church that went against the ideals of Christianity; the poverty, obedience and chastity that made up the vocation of the monk were by no means universally upheld. But this does not mean that Chaucer saw the Church as a whole as corrupt. Indeed, this was far from the case. The Parson, for example, is the model of the good Christian minister, just as the Ploughman is the model of the good, ordinary Christian working in the world. It is when we compare these model characters to the Pardoner that we can see something of the range of the medieval Catholic Church and Chaucer's response to it. Where the Parson is poor, devout and honest, the Pardoner is corrupt, money-seeking and dishonest. He is a sad, worldly character, a hypocrite and, as his Tale reveals, a drunkard.

But, for all its worldliness and corruption of faith, the Church bound medieval society together. Even the Pardoner, in his attempts to make money, has to inspire faith in his congregation (see pp. 37–9). He does good despite himself. From the top of society to the lowest dregs, Christianity provided an inspiration, a solace, a vocation and an income. For the best it provided a sense of duty and a vision of salvation. The Knight, for example, the epitome of the top of the feudal hierarchy at its best, goes on crusades to fight against the Moslems. The Ploughman digs and delves for the love of poor neighbours. Finally, the Church even provides a role in life for the Summoner and the Pardoner.

Most importantly, all the characters in the poem have come together ostensibly for a religious purpose. It is spring. Love and faith have been rekindled after the deadness and dreariness of winter (a season far harsher for the people of the medieval period who lived without the comforts we take for granted). Spring is the time for a communal affirmation of faith. Of course, the depth and sincerity of this varies from individual to individual. The Knight goes on his pilgrimage immediately after his journeys abroad. The Wife of Bath – an inveterate pilgrim – clearly enjoys the travelling and the chance it gives her to meet and gossip with other people. Perhaps she will even find a new lover. To the Pardoner, the pilgrimage is an excuse to make money by plying his trade to a captive audience.

Here, then, is the widest cross-section of medieval society. We see the high-born and the lowly, the young and the middle-aged, the innocents and the villains, the devout and the worldly, the sincere and the hypocritical. Nonetheless, it is the Church and the ideal of religious service that has drawn them all together.

The pilgrimage also provided Chaucer with a narrative framework for his stories. Collections of tales were popular in the Middle Ages. A famous Italian example which we know Chaucer was familiar with was the *Decameron* of Giovanni Boccaccio. In this a group of nobles, retreating from their city at a time of plague, tell stories to while away the time. Chaucer, as we have seen, was a poet who wrote chiefly for the court, but the wealth and genius of the *Canterbury Tales* lies in his daring to extend his art from the enclosed, refined world of the aristocracy into the more commonplace areas of society. As John Dryden, another great English poet, wrote of them: 'Here indeed is God's plenty.'

Chaucer himself was uniquely placed to appreciate the wealth of human life around him. He was born in London somewhere around the year 1340 and, at an early age, was placed as a pageboy in the magnificently colourful and courtly household of the Countess of Ulster. In 1357 there is a record of a payment made for the cloak and multi-coloured tights he was required to wear. Thus, although not born into the aristocracy, he early learned the ways of their world and knew from close observation the lives of such as the Knight and the Squire. As a young man he would have learned French and Latin, eventually adding Italian to this. He would also have learned the ways of poetry and have begun to find his vocation as a poet.

Not that Chaucer's experience was limited to the gorgeous and ceremonious life of the English court. He fought as a soldier in France, was captured and ransomed, the King himself contributing to his release. He eventually married – we know very little about his wife – and, because of his energy and intelligence (and, no doubt, his gift for languages) he was soon being sent on diplomatic missions to France, Italy and Flanders. In 1374 he was appointed a Controller of Customs at the Port of London. Perhaps it was here or on his journeys that he met the originals of such characters as the Shipman. And, like the Sergeant of the Law, Chaucer was increasing his wealth through his skills. By 1385, he had, like the Franklin, become a Justice of the Peace, and soon afterwards he was to become a Member of Parliament. After briefly falling victim to the political turmoil of his time, Chaucer re-entered court life and was given a number of jobs such as Chief Forester and Controller of the King's Works. These furthered his experience of men and the professions they followed.

Thus, like many of the pilgrims, Chaucer himself was a busy professional man, but the portrait we have given so far only suggests that he was a successful and, no doubt, ambitious civil-servant. It gives no reason to suspect that he was probably the greatest poet in the English language before Shakespeare. Indeed, he ranks among the greatest poets of all time.

It is clear that Chaucer had an immensely vigorous and receptive mind. He was interested in everything around him. He was fascinated by the scientific knowledge of his day and was widely read in many areas. He wrote about philosophy and astronomy, while his description of the Doctor shows his interest in medicine. He was also widely versed in the literature of the Continent, especially in the most recent poetic developments in France and Italy. This can be seen in many of his earlier works. Above all, however, he had rich experience of people and the way in which they lived. He was observant and sometimes critical, but the *Canterbury Tales* and, in particular, the portraits in the *General Prologue*, show a wise and kind delicacy of heart, an intuitive understanding of all sorts and conditions of people. Chaucer can be wry and even ironic, but he is never cynical. He knows a rogue when he meets one, but he usually has a good word for him. Those he admired – like the Knight, the Parson and the Ploughman – he presents with great dignity and an easy sense of respect. Above all, perhaps, Chaucer was warmed by people who lived fully and shared their life with others, people who were richly human even if they were flawed. For this reason

– if for no other – the difficulties of his language, the strangeness of his world and some of his ideas are worth tackling and coming to understand, for Chaucer has the gift of the supreme artist: he makes us feel more fully alive.

CHAUCER'S LANGUAGE

Language, like all things, changes and develops. No one was more aware of this than Chaucer. In his great poem *Troilus and Criseyde* he prays that all the people of his time will be able to read his work and understand him. This may seem rather strange at first, but, as Chaucer explains, medieval people spoke different dialects of English in different parts of the country. When we study Chaucer's language, we are looking at the origins of the English we ourselves speak and read. This alone makes it fascinating.

The dialect of English in which Chaucer wrote was that spoken in the most prosperous and powerful parts of the country: London and the East Midlands. As it developed, so it became the dominant form of the tongue. The grammar and vocabulary of Middle English (as the English of Chaucer's day is called) was drawn from French, Latin and the native Anglo-Saxon. French was the dominant language of the court. Latin was the language of the Church Anglo-Saxon had been spoken before the Norman Conquest and survived amongst the majority of people, though changing all the time. This wealth of influences on the language made Chaucer's English both rich and flexible.

It also appears difficult at first. Do not be frightened by this and do not think either that you can get by with just a translation. You cannot. You must be able to read Chaucer in the original.

It is possible, of course, to set out the rules of Chaucer's grammar in a table which can be learnt by heart. But, aside from being a very dull exercise, this is neither necessary nor a particularly satisfactory procedure. It is far better to become familiar with Chaucer's English by listening to it, reading it to yourself, and absorbing its forms almost unconsciously. After all, that is probably how you learnt to speak English in the first place. As you become more familiar with Chaucer's language in this way a number of grammatical forms we no longer use will strike you. For example, we learn that the pilgrims had 'by aventure *y-falle*' in company. The 'y' is one method of making a past participle. We would say 'fallen'. Another example of this form is the Shipman's boat which 'ycleped was the Maudelayne'. 'Clepen' means 'to be called' and we meet it in the description of the Prioress when we are told that her name is Madam Eglentyne. Nonetheless – and just to show you that the rules of grammar were far from fixed – the actual line in which Chaucer gives her name reads: 'And she was cleped madame Eglentyne.' Chaucer has abandoned the 'y' and put 'ed' on the end, just as we would.

Something else you should look out for is the way Chaucer makes a negative statement. He says of the Knight:

> 'He never yet no vileinye ne sayde
> In al his lyf, un-to no maner wight.'

A literal translation might read: 'He had never yet not said nothing ill-bred to no one in all his life.' Chaucer here has used a double negative, but unlike modern English the meaning remains negative: 'He had never yet said anything ill-bred to anyone in his whole life.' Chaucer might well have pointed out that that was the way negatives were made in the French his contemporaries spoke. If you read Chaucer's words carefully, the sense is quite obvious.

Chaucer's grammar usually presents fewer problems than his vocabulary. Here there is no substitute for conscientiously learning what the words mean. The best way of going about this – and probably the one you are using in class – is to take a single paragraph or portrait and work through it systematically. You'll find some words that have not changed. If we look at the lines from the description of the Knight quoted above, 'he', 'his', 'yet', 'no', 'in' and 'un-to' present no problems. 'Lyf' is obvious enough, so are 'maner' and 'sayde'. You will thus need to look up only two words: 'wight' and 'vileinye'. The first means 'a living person' and, incidentally, comes from Anglo-Saxon. The second presents a special but common problem and is an example of something you must be careful of. 'Vileinye' means 'the behaviour of a villein' and 'villein' is a feudal term for a peasant. It is a word that has a precise meaning but refers to a way of life that has now wholly disappeared. It is an interesting example of how the meaning of a word can change over the centuries – it is, of course, the Middle English ancestor of our word 'villain'. You should be familiar with other words of this type: 'gentil', 'Yeoman', 'Knight of the Shire', 'anlas', 'gipser', 'vernicle'. These are all words that refer to now more or less obsolete forms of behaviour, institutions or objects. Being sure of what they mean will, however, bring you closer to understanding Chaucer's real world. To know exactly what they mean is to appreciate something of the life and colour of the world in which Chaucer wrote.

But be careful: do not think you know the meaning of a word simply because you can guess at its modern equivalent. Let us look at the line from which 'gentil' comes:

'He was a verray parfit, gentil knight.'

This does *not* mean: 'He was a very perfect, delicate knight.' Nor does it mean that he was 'perfectly gentle'. 'Gentil' is what a gentleman is. It indicates a consideration for others that goes with good breeding. 'Parfit' means 'complete' or 'finished' and therefore 'as good as possible'. It is the idea of completion that Chaucer is stressing here, as in the phrase: 'I have now perfected (or completed) my plans.' In other words, the knight is the *complete* gentleman.

A lot of words Chaucer uses have fallen into disuse and have been replaced by others: 'tretys', 'soothly', 'corages' are all examples of these. They are words you must look up and learn. An attempt to translate a passage into good modern English will soon show you (and the examiners) whether you have really done your homework or are just bluffing.

In summary, what you are doing is this: listening to and reading the text, following the grammar and examining every word to see if it refers to a now obsolete form of behaviour, institution or object, checking whether it has the same meaning today as it had in Chaucer's time, and finally, if it is an obsolete word, learning what it means. You must do this conscientiously and regularly. Try not to tackle many more than twenty lines at a session.

Finally to pronunciation. You must make every effort to hear Chaucer spoken either in class or on a record, or both. Imitation is the only way of achieving correct pronunciation and you will find

Chaucer's poetry much easier to appreciate if you speak it properly. A number of guidelines may be useful here.

First comes Chaucer's spelling. This was not fixed in his day. As a result it is largely phonetic: in other words you should usually pronounce all the letters, including the final 'e'. (Incidentally, this is *not* pronounced like the first 'e' of 'even' but more like the second one in 'ever'.) However do not pronounce the final 'e' of a word if the word that follows begins with a vowel.

If you read Chaucer in this way you will soon see how rich his vowel sounds are. But the consonants too are stressed in a different way from ours. We may take 'knight' as an example. We still preserve the 'gh' in our spelling of 'knight' but we don't pronounce it. The same is true of the 'k'. Chaucer put them in because he *did* pronounce them. His 'knight' is nearly a two-syllable word. The first part sounds something like 'cur', the second like the German 'nicht'. One way of checking this is to scan the line.

The majority of Chaucer's lines have ten syllables in a regular pattern. Syllables you emphasize usually alternate with those you don't. Thus:

'Whan that Aprille with his shourés soté'

If you do not sound the 'e' in 'shourés' and 'soté' then there are quite simply not enough syllables to fill up the line. This becomes obvious when you read it out aloud.

As you become familiar with Chaucer's language you will see how rich all its sounds are. These notes are designed only to start you off, but remember: the surest way to understand Chaucer's English is to hear it being read out loud while you follow it in your text and then try to translate it for yourself.

THE PILGRIMS

The Knight (43–78)

Chaucer's Knight personifies the virtues of medieval chivalry. He is a brave and active soldier, but he is far more than a mere war-machine. His values include things other than prowess. He is, for example, a man of honour and integrity. He values liberal behaviour and good manners. He does not brag or boast. Rather, he is a man of exceptional modesty. He has never been discourteous to anyone in his life. In other words, he is a gentleman.

The Knight is the pilgrim of highest social status. As such, he sets an example of good breeding and illustrates many of the ideals of behaviour that were fundamental to the medieval world. As we have seen (see pp. 8–9), the medieval world was – generally speaking – feudal. This meant there was a fairly strict hierarchy or system of social grades. Those like the Knight who were close to the top of it were supposed to inspire others in three related areas: war, religious faith, and everyday behaviour.

Chaucer shows his Knight to have been particularly active in war. He has travelled extensively, his exploits taking him to both ends of the Mediterranean and into the Baltic countries. In these last, English knights regularly fought on a mercenary basis. Here, as everywhere, the Knight has greatly distinguished himself and has been given the place of honour at banquets.

It is also clear that much of the Knight's experience of warfare has been gained in fighting Moorish forces. During this period the energetic and highly civilized kingdoms of the Moslems had greatly extended their influence, particularly in the Holy Land. It was, therefore, the duty of a Christian fighting man to repel them – to be a Crusader. The Knight has followed this calling in countries as far apart as Spain and Turkey. All of these campaigns were of course the great international struggles of the time involving many thousands of men, but Chaucer also shows the Knight having fought three tournaments against a single heathen adversary, slaying him on each occasion. Knighthood and Christian faith are here combined.

The way the Knight conducts himself again reflects this combination of honour and Christian humility. Deadly as a professional soldier though he is, the Knight is not a loud-mouthed and dangerous braggart. In fact, he is quite the reverse. We are told that he is courteous, meek and – the sign of a true gentleman – considerate to all people, regardless of their social status.

These qualities of modesty are reflected in the way the Knight is dressed. He is not extravagant and his surcoat is dirtied from his armour. This shows at once his active pursuit of his calling (and note that he is careful to provide himself with good horses for this) and also the sincerity of his religious convictions. He has come directly from an expedition but, rather than spruce himself up, he has gone at once on a pilgrimage to give thanks to God. Such professionalism, sincerity and faithfulness are things Chaucer deeply respected.

The Knight is an international figure. The only other pilgrim who has travelled anywhere near as far is (rather surprisingly) the Wife of Bath. This breadth of experience, coupled with his breeding, makes the Knight a natural leader. Harry Bailey, who is a full-blooded extrovert, realizes this. It is the Knight whom he asks to draw the first straw when the telling of tales is about to begin and, as it happens, the Knight wins the privilege of telling the first story. Note how willingly he does so. He is not in the least grand or pompous about it. He is cheerfully dutiful. He also happens to tell an exceptionally fine story.

The Squire (79–100)

The ideal aristocrats of the Middle Ages did not just live in the world of religious and military duty. The younger nobleman in particular developed a highly sophisticated code of behaviour centred around love. This is personified in the Squire. He is youthful and passionate. Indeed, he is so ardently in love that he cannot sleep at night. It is his desire to display himself to advantage before his lady that lies behind all he does. His clothes, for example, are lavish and in the height of fashion. Not for him is his father's soiled surcoat. Rather, he wears a short gown with long wide sleeves. It must have looked something like the one Chaucer had brought for him when he was a pageboy (see p. 11). However, the whole is stiff with embroidery. Chaucer makes a mild joke of this, but it is not an unkind one. Furthermore, the flowers stitched all over his short gown and the way Chaucer compares him to a nightingale serve to make him at one with the invocation of spring at the start of the poem. Winter and decay are over. The sap is rising. The heart begins to beat faster and love and potency have been restored. What better way to suggest this than through a young man in love.

Many of the skills of the young courtier were displayed to enhance his lovelife. Courting ladies was the activity of courtly young men. To this end the Squire has learned to write and draw, play music and make up lyrics. All of these activities were the legitimate, youthful skills expected from a fashionable young man.

Over-dressed and amorous though he is, the Squire is not feeble. He may seem to curl his hair (no fashion is really new) but Chaucer tells us directly that he is both agile and very strong: a fledgling soldier who has so far only seen service in northern Europe. Nonetheless, he has distinguished himself. The Squire knows how to joust and ride his horse properly, and we get the impression that more experience will make a good soldier of him. We see, too, that he has something of the enduring qualities of his father. The Squire is not a rebellious adolescent He is modest and obedient, well aware of the behaviour that is expected of him in the adult world and willing to abide by it. It is these aspects of his character – his willingness to be of service – that Chaucer leaves us with.

The Yeoman (101–117)

Both the Squire and the Yeoman are servants to the Knight. The Yeoman is an example of something Chaucer particularly admired: professional skill. The Yeoman has the solid dignity of the true craftsman. He knows everything about forestry. But notice how Chaucer achieves this effect. All that we know of the Yeoman's appearance is that he has close-cropped hair and a brown face. All our other impressions come from his equipment: his green forester's clothes, his sharp, shining and well-maintained arrows, his bow and bracer, his somewhat fancy dagger which is, nonetheless, as sharp as a spear. Here is a man who is honest and fulfilled in his place in life. Yet he is far from lacking personality. The greens of his clothes and the colourful flights of his arrows are cheerful, while the shining silver medallion of St Christopher (his patron saint) is both a showy and a cheerful thing as well as a sign of his faith and his devotion to his craft.

And his craft is something that Chaucer would have known and appreciated from personal experience (see pp. 11–12).

The Prioress (118–164)

The Prioress is a rather more complex figure than the Knight and his entourage. It is her little weaknesses that seem to make her an individual. Where the accoutrements of the Yeoman show a person completely at one with his place in life, Chaucer's description of the Prioress with, among other things, her wimple neatly pleated and her little dogs is mildly but kindly critical.

The Prioress is, above all things, a lady. She would like to be considered a great lady. Her table-manners are exceptionally refined. She does not spill food down herself. (This was, remember, the period before the introduction of forks and a time when decorous behaviour was the exception rather than the rule.) She does not allow herself to be seen with a greasy mouth or to snatch at her food. Rather she tries to impress people with her delicacy and her bearing so that she will be thought all the more worthy of respect.

It takes some tact on our part to describe the Prioress's behaviour accurately. It is not fair to accuse her of snobbery. The Prioress is too pure and simple a woman for this. Her behaviour is best seen as a harmless form of worldliness.

Her rather sentimental emotions could be seen as a result of her over-refinement and her fairly sheltered life. She spoils her little dogs, pampering them with the most costly food. She cries when they are ill-treated or when she sees a mouse caught in a trap.

The way in which she is dressed increases our impression of her harmless worldliness. As a nun, she was obliged, of course, to wear a habit. But notice the little vanities of her dress: the finely pleated wimple, her rosary (which is as much a piece of jewellery as an aid to prayer) and her exposed forehead which should be covered.

The Prioress has been brought up as a member of the English aristocracy. That is why – like them – she speaks Anglo-French. This is the language that developed out of the French brought to England by William the Conqueror (see p. 13). It is no criticism of her that she speaks French with this regional accent. It merely indicates her nationality and social status: she is an upper-class English woman. And it is social status the Prioress insists on. She is as much a lady as she is a nun. As a lady, she retains her little worldly vanities and indulgences: her dogs (which, strictly speaking, she should not have owned), her manners, her deportment, her interest in clothes and jewellery. It would be very uncharitable to say such pleasures are wrong. Chaucer is much more kindly and broad-minded than that. He is amused and rather touched by this big-boned spinster clinging to the manners of the court he knew so well.

You should notice that Chaucer does not ever say that the Prioress has no religious vocation. She is introduced to us as modest and Chaucer does tell us that she sings and intones the mass beautifully. She lends her refinement of feeling to the worship of God. In addition, her jewellery is of a more or less religious nature: a rosary and a brooch with a religious motto. There is no real reason to think that *Amor vincit omnia* refers to anything but love of God. Any suggestion to the contrary must be carefully weighed against our own unfamiliarity with an England steeped in the pervasive and powerful influence of religion and the Catholic Church.

In essence, then, the Prioress is a refined and ladylike creature, well-bred and keen to make clear to all that she is just this. She has her little, harmless, worldly vanities but, again, she does bring delicacy and refinement both to those around her and to the religious life she lives.

Like the Knight – and as befits her sex and social status – the Prioress has servants in attendance: her chaplain and three priests. It is one of these priests who tells the delightful *Nun's Priest's Tale*.

The Monk (165–207)

The worldliness of the Church is clear in the portrait of the Monk; but, just as Chaucer's criticisms of the Prioress are tempered with much good humour and warmth of heart, so here Chaucer avoids condemning the Monk outright. He is described as a physical and very masculine man. In effective contrast to the Prioress and her little dogs, it is energy and activity that Chaucer stresses here. The Monk's job takes him out of his cloister. His eyes roll about his head which blazes like the fire under a cauldron. He has a healthy (not to say rather self-indulgent) appetite. This last, of course, is a criticism. The Monk is certainly worldly. He is, above all, a hunting man, and hunting was forbidden to members of the clergy. This one, however, keeps a stable of fine horses and, appropriately for a man of his gusto, he has loudly jingling harnesses. His hounds are as swift as flying birds.

Clearly, the Monk is a man of some substance. The monastic ideal of poverty had become, in many cases, no more than a matter of lip-service at this time. The Monk spends a great deal of money on hunting, and his clothes – like those of the Prioress – show signs of worldliness. His sleeves have expensive fur at the wrist and he wears a gold brooch with a love-knot on it.

The Monk could not be said to follow the true monastic vocation: the upholding of the vows of poverty, obedience and chastity. He is not poor, he is far from obedient – Chaucer tells us directly that the Monk considered the older monastic rules too strict and out of date – while his brooch casts some doubt on his chastity. The Monk does not see himself as a poor, quiet scholar, nor as a man suited to labouring for the love of God. We might compare him in this respect to the Ploughman. The Monk asks what good such self-denial does the world. And Chaucer, it seems, agrees with him, though we cannot discount the possibility that he is being ironic. It is important to realize that line 183 (and other sharp criticisms of Church corruption) does not indicate that Chaucer was anti-religious in any way. There is no question of his being anything other than a devout man, but, like all intelligent people of his time, he was well aware of abuses in the Church (particularly in the monastic orders) and he was not afraid to point them out. His portraits of the Parson and the Ploughman make his respect for the truly devout absolutely clear and you should always consider them when discussing Chaucer's criticism of abuses in the religious life.

The Friar (208–271)

The Friar is a complete rogue. Chaucer makes no bones about this. He tells us at the start that he is a flatterer and a gossip, a man whose marrying off of young women is not an act of charity but, by implication, a discreet way of removing discarded girlfriends. He cultivates the rich and the attractive and, far worse, abuses his power of granting confession by making such things easy for those who pay him well. His motives in life are pleasure and, even more importantly, profit. What makes him so engaging is the fact that his hypocrisy is so audacious. He relies on the belief that giving money to poor orders is a sign that a man is truly repentant. He says that some men are so hard-hearted that they cannot weep for their sins even if they want to – such men, in his view, redeem themselves equally well by offering the Friars their cash. As a religious and moral stance this is dubious at best. The Friar, however, is so obviously more interested in sinners' money than in the state of their souls that, in his hands, moral values collapse almost completely.

In addition, the Friar is wholly given over to worldly pleasures. He carries round with him a generous supply of little love-gifts to give to the housewives whom, it is perhaps suggested, he would like to seduce. Further, he pursues the local owners of public houses, is a considerable performer of popular songs and is obnoxiously servile to the wealthy and influential. Not only does he court the rich and the powerful but, at the same time, he is not above tricking money out of the poorest and most gullible. Struggling widows will give him their hard-earned farthings. Charity – the love of the poor and the sickly – is something the Friar cannot practise. His worldliness has hardened his heart. Those who most deserve his compassion – the lepers and the beggars – he has no time for. After all, they cannot advance his career nor make him money. He has supposedly given his life over to poverty and an imitation of the ways of Christ, yet he mixes with inn-keepers because he likes drinking and shuns those who most need help. He pays to keep his patch clear of other friars and thus guarantees all the rich pickings for himself. We are given to understand that he makes a very comfortable living from these. He is well-dressed, worldly and affected. He is a gossip, a snob and a disgrace to the Church.

How is it, then, that Chaucer does not condemn him out of hand? The answer is that, while appreciating how wrong the Friar is, Chaucer's gusto and enthusiasm, his fascination with someone so outrageously corrupt, is stronger than his anger. Hubert (and it is interesting that Chaucer gives the Friar a name) is, above all things, alive. We know that he is wrong. We are clearly shown that he is so. But we cannot despise him completely without appearing rather superior and foolish ourselves. And, finally, the Friar is redeemed for us by a touch of poetry that even he is probably not aware of. Sinful and worldly though he is, there is something so engrossing about his eyes twinkling like stars in the frosty night as he sings his love songs, that we have to smile and almost forgive him even as we shake our heads in disapproval. Though he can be sharp, Chaucer's heart is too rich and understanding to condemn anyone utterly. It is for this sort of mature and humane sympathy that we read him.

The Merchant (272–286)

It is interesting to compare the portraits of the Friar and the Merchant. Both, in varying degrees, are rogues but, whereas Hubert is somehow excused by his sheer vitality, the anonymous Merchant leaves a slightly sour taste. He is well-dressed, pompous and devious. He has a bee in his bonnet about the safety of shipping routes, indulges in black-market currency speculations and skilfully hides the fact that he is in debt.

It is unusual for Chaucer not to admire professional skills, even dishonest ones – and the Merchant's skills are clearly considerable. It is often said that Chaucer's comment that he cannot remember the Merchant's name is a slur on the man – a courtly poet's rather condescending dismissal of a member of the middle classes. This may be so. What is interesting, however, is Chaucer's creation of a faceless businessman, a narrow and self-obsessed man who clearly does nothing to enhance the vitality of those around him.

The Clerk (287–310)

The Clerk is the 'eternal student', poor and unworldly, but clearly a type Chaucer had sympathy for. After all, the Clerk is an idealist and he is a man of real worth.

His poverty is what first impresses us. He is thin, his horse is thinner and his clothes are threadbare. He is the true intellectual, wholly given over to the unprofitable pursuit of scholarship. He has not got himself a job in the Church and he is quite unsuitable for a post in the world of affairs. The Clerk has to beg money from friends and patrons. All that he gets he spends on books. He repays it not in kind but by praying for his benefactors' souls. This is the first wholly sincere example of the Christian life we have seen since we met the Knight.

Chaucer jokingly compares the Clerk and his love of true philosophy to the alchemists – the 'natural philosophers', who pursued wealth by searching for a means to turn base metal into gold. All these men succeeded in doing was making themselves poor. The Clerk's studies have made him no more wealthy than these men. However, Chaucer's joke here is not a harsh one. The impression we are left with is of someone wholly (almost hopelessly) sincere, with a true dignity about him. The Clerk's religion is as genuine as his devotion to scholarship. This gives him a certain bearing of which he is probably unaware: a combination of intelligence, honesty and moral dignity which he unselfconsciously shares with others. This Chaucer deeply respects. He shows him as a man who is both willing to pass on the knowledge that he has and to learn what he can from other people. This sense of sharing and communal life was something Chaucer valued very greatly.

The Sergeant of the Law (311–332)

One of the most fascinating things about the *General Prologue* is Chaucer's dramatic juxtaposition of his pilgrims and the little groups they form amongst themselves. A good example of this is the friendship of the Sergeant of the Law (or Barrister) and the Franklin, and the way in which these two stand in contrast to the Clerk who precedes them and the Guildsmen who come after them.

Chaucer, as we have seen, had a great respect for professionalism and craftsmanship. The Knight, the Yeoman and the Clerk possess both these qualities. Even the Friar rouses a certain sneaking admiration. The Sergeant of the Law, too, is not an insignificant man. He has real expertise and, quite rightly, has earned a lot of money from it. He has the considerable, rather cool intelligence of a top professional man, and if Chaucer can have a joke at his expense – his pretence of being furiously busy all the time – that does not mean that he despises him. Why not? It is partly because his knowledge is truly impressive. His skills inspire confidence and he is richly experienced.

Again, we are given no very clear idea of what he looked like. We are told that his clothes are not particularly pretentious. The band of silk round his waist is a vivid detail. But, like many of the pilgrims, the Sergeant of the Law is chiefly defined by what he is, by his profession and his skills. But there is one further point we should notice. We are told that he uses his money to buy up land. He is, in other words, securing his place as a landed gentleman and he does this with the money that he has earned from the exercise of his talents. This is interesting in the light of Chaucer's portrait of the Sergeant of the Law's friend, the Franklin.

The Franklin (333–362)

The Franklin is a splendid character: prosperous and pleasure-loving, with an intelligent and active feeling for his social responsibilities. His daisy-white beard, outgoing disposition and generosity inspire admiration for this elderly, well-adjusted man who lives life to the full. Notice how Chaucer delights in detail here – the silk purse, the beard, the sword and, even more, the lavish provision of food and drink the Franklin insists on. Indeed, Chaucer says it snows down in his house with all the good things a man can think of.

But such plenty as this is not mere random abundance. Pleasure may be the Franklin's aim in life, but he sets about securing it in an organized way. His cook has to work very hard and is told off severely if he is not up to the mark. There is, to be sure, a side to the Franklin that is generous and extrovert, but he is not simply a jolly Father-Christmas-like figure. He is concerned about quality and the efficient running of his household. His wine-cellar is carefully stocked, his stew ponds are well maintained, his birds are put out to fatten in the proper way. His dining-table is orderly.

Thus, for all his sense of pleasure, the Franklin is a man who values proper organization and makes sure that he gets it. This implies a strong personality and considerable intelligence. These qualities are underlined when we look at the duties he has taken on at various times: Justice of the Peace, Member of Parliament, Sheriff and Shire Accountant. All of these were responsible positions requiring energy, organization and a sense of duty and responsibility. Here they seem to stem quite naturally from the Franklin's prosperous and extrovert nature. We see that he is not simply a pleasure-seeker, but also a man of vigour and intelligence. This impression is enhanced by his friendship with the Sergeant of the Law, whom we have learned to respect for his intelligence and his experience. We have seen that he is buying his way into the landed gentry. In many ways, the Franklin complements this. He already has his lands, his established position, and he uses his leisure to undertake responsible social duties. What both men have in common is wealth, intelligence and a willingness to participate in justice and the law. They are the two pilgrims who represent the rising English middle classes: shrewd, responsible and wealthy. They are men of substance who can be trusted and, Chaucer suggests, admired.

The Guildsmen (363–380)

The five Guildsmen are members of the citizen classes. They too are rich, but, unlike the Sergeant of the Law and the Franklin, they are not particularly interested in public service.

Chaucer presents them with mild satire, rather in the way he does the Merchant, who is another member of the citizen class. Like him, they are not particularly distinctive as characters. Perhaps as a parallel, they are all dressed in the same way – they wear the livery of a great and solemn fraternity. Maybe Chaucer is poking fun at this rather humourless pomp.

The five men are certainly rich. Chaucer tells us that each of them has enough money to be the alderman or chief of his guild. (The 'fraternity' they belong to is not the same as their trade guild – each man would have been a member of a different guild and worn a different livery. The 'fraternity' is probably a religious or charitable foundation.) Of course, in terms of the City of London, all the guilds of craftsmen were important and powerful. They regulated the City's trading life and looked after members' interests. The position of alderman of a guild carried considerable prestige. It still does.

But Chaucer's satire is not only at the expense of the somewhat introverted and faceless nature of these men. He shows that they are keen to show off the wealth they have made. Their ornate knives and purses are status symbols whose modern equivalents might be expensive cuff-links or thick gold signet rings. It is worth remembering, however, that the Middle Ages was a period of much greater display than ours. Personal adornment, particularly among the wealthy, was far more widespread than it is now. We need only to look again at the Yeoman and the Squire to see this. Indeed, so great was the allure of displaying wealth through dress that laws had to be passed regulating it. The silver caps on these men's knives are an indication of their money, and an expression of their social position.

But Chaucer reserves his most telling satire for his description of their wives. Here is a wonderful insight into bossy, bourgeois snobbery. These women quite clearly drive their husbands on to success and are desperately concerned about their own social status. Their whole ambition in life is to queen it in front of their contemporaries, to be called 'Madam' – a courtesy title – and to have their trains borne by a page. Their equivalents today would perhaps demand a huge car and a mink coat. It is such insights as these into the unchanging types of human life that make the *General Prologue* so vivid.

The Cook (381–389)

The Cook that the Guildsmen have brought with them is a strange character. We later discover that his connoisseur's interest in London ale is more than a professional skill. He has succumbed to his occupation's chief hazard: he is a drunkard. This does not mean he is not highly proficient at his job. Chaucer takes his usual delight in describing the skills of the Cook's trade and suggesting the man's excellence through them. But it is the vivid detail of the growth on his shin – something particularly nauseating considering his job – that brings the Cook most memorably alive. He is much more distinctive than his guildsmen employers.

The Shipman (390–412)

Here is an odd character to find on a pilgrimage. The Shipman, who has come from the far West Country, is a rogue whom Chaucer clearly found rather admirable. Perhaps he had met a figure like him when he was a customs inspector (see p. 12).

We see him riding rather awkwardly. He has a suntanned face and we are told later that he has survived many storms. Chaucer paints him particularly vividly by contrasting three aspects of his personality: his dishonesty, his love of winning a good fight, and, most important as always, his professional competence. We are told that the Shipman's boat – the *Magdalene* – is often hired out to the wine trade running between England and Bordeaux and that the Shipman has, on many occasions, stolen some of the cargo for himself. Further, in a time when the seas were not safe (we recall the Merchant's wish to have them kept free from pirates, regardless of cost), he has been involved in fights and, when he has won, has drowned his enemies. Perhaps he was even something of a pirate himself. There is no suggestion that his fighting was always merely a matter of self-defence. Chaucer leaves the matter ambiguous and lets us draw our own conclusions.

What does raise Chaucer's respect, however, is the Shipman's knowledge of his craft, his skills at navigation, his experience, and his intimate knowledge of the coasts of Brittany and Spain. For all his roguishness, we feel that here is a man who is an expert in his field.

The Physician (413–446)

Here is another man of considerable professional skill who is, again, something of a rogue. However, when discussing the Physician, it is important to remember that his 'natural magic', his grounding in astronomy or astrology (the two were interchangeable terms) and his belief in the theory of the humours were all wholly acceptable at the time. More than this, they formed the basis of medieval science about which Chaucer was very knowledgeable.

Chaucer tells us that the Physician preserves the lives of his patients (something that was not invariably the case) and is skilful at foretelling the moment when the planets arc (in astrological terms) most favourable towards his patient. This is the time, too, when the images the Physician has made either of the sick man or of the relevant signs of the Zodiac will be most effective. Here was an area of expertise learned from Arabic medicine and, as we shall see, the Physician is well-read in Arabic sources.

He is also familiar with the theory of the four humours and we must share something of his knowledge if we are to understand his skills. It was believed that men's differing temperaments were the result of differing combinations of the four humours. These were liquids named melancholy (or black bile), phlegm, blood and yellow bile (or choler). Each was held to come from a particular organ of the body and, like everything else, it was believed that each humour was in its turn made up from combinations of two of the four basic qualities of hot, cold, moist and dry. Thus melancholy was cold and dry, phlegm was cold and moist, blood was hot and moist and yellow bile was hot and dry. The predominating humour controlled a man's complexion, or temperament. We still sometimes describe people as melancholic, phlegmatic, sanguine or choleric. We have seen that the Franklin had a sanguine temperament. In other words sanguine (or blood) was his dominant humour. This made him a vigorous, extrovert man. The Reeve, on the other hand, is described as a choleric person. He is sour tempered. A man remained in good health all the time his combination of humours was in balance. As soon as the balance was upset, however, it was believed a man fell ill and, in the hope of reducing the excess humour, his blood was let. Chaucer says that the Physician is an expert in knowing what form of imbalance in the humours has led to his patient's particular disease and what part of his body was responsible for this. This formed his diagnosis. When it was complete – and the astrological signs were favourable – the Physician could hope to cure him.

To help with the cure the Physician had apothecaries to make up his medicines for him. It is important to remember that to Chaucer the theory of the humours was an acceptable explanation of illness. It may seem bogus to us. It was not to him. However, when it comes to the apothecaries, Chaucer does see signs of trickery and dishonest dealing. It was not a new criticism to see that the Physician favours the apothecaries with work and he in turn benefits from them. Both parties have known each other for a long time and have clearly made a lot of money from their mutual acquaintance. All this, of course, was at the patient's expense.

But, for all this, the Physician is a knowledgeable man. Chaucer takes a great delight in naming all the specialists the Physician has studied: beginning with the legendary Greek founder of medicine Aesculapius and going on to later Greek, Persian, Arabic and more contemporary doctors.

If the Physician is knowledgeable, he is also sensible. Chaucer tells us that he is at pains to keep himself fit by eating a moderate but healthy diet. Perhaps the Physician appreciated how dangerous it was to go to the doctor! The Physician is not particularly fond of the Bible (such men were generally thought to be sceptical scientists rather than faithful Christians) and his real love is love of money. His rich, silk-lined clothes show that he is a wealthy man and Chaucer comments that he does particularly well in times of plague. Just as gold helps cure sick men, so it is a tonic to the Physician's purse as well. For this reason, he loves gold.

The Wife of Bath (447–478)

The Wife of Bath is one of the great characters of English literature. Ageing, worldly, vulgar and amorous, she has been married five times and is on the look out for a sixth husband. She gives us more information about her lives and loves – indeed, a great deal more – in the *Prologue* to her own Tale. We find out there, for example, why she is slightly deaf – her fourth husband hit her when, one day, she snatched a book he was reading about the sinfulness of women out of his hands.

The Wife herself is rich, a skilled weaver, and jealous of her social position. The Church is never simply a place of worship for her. It provides an opportunity for her to display her standing (something which she is most insistent about) and, as she tells us in her *Prologue*, it is a place where she can watch the men. Pilgrimage provided her with an opportunity for travelling (it is curious that, aside from the Knight and perhaps the Shipman, she is probably the most widely travelled of all the pilgrims) and meeting people. She has been to Jerusalem no less than three times, to Rome, Boulogne-sur-mer, Cologne and to the most famous of all pilgrim shrines, the Cathedral of St James at Compostella. Such excessive indulgence in pilgrimages was not favourably viewed by the Church. The clerics knew too well that mere travel detracted from the essentially serious purpose of pilgrimage. It is also worth recalling that such journeys were both arduous and dangerous. They help to show that the Wife is clearly a robust and adventurous woman, but Chaucer suggests that all these 'wanderings' also entailed moral straying from the straight and narrow. With charming tact he suggests that the Wife of Bath had known men before her marriage, but he stops himself from a full revelation by saying that this is neither the time nor the place to talk about such things.

The widely spaced teeth which the Wife of Bath possesses were held by some to indicate a love of travel. She herself calls them a sign of her amorous nature. Chaucer concludes the portrait by saying that she perhaps knew something about love-potions and was well experienced in all that appertains to love.

There could, perhaps, have been something rather pathetic about this ageing, amorous woman with her astonishingly vulgar outfit: her huge hat and swathes of wimples, her bright red stockings and mantle over her broad hips. In fact, this is not at all the impression we are left with. Like so many of the characters Chaucer relishes, the Wife of Bath has the vigorous, extroverted and sociable nature that he loved. Alison, as she is called, exudes so much energy, so much sheer life. Of course she is mildly ridiculous and she is certainly no better than she ought to be, but through all of this, her bursts of laughter and anger, her sheer raucous physical presence, we feel the influence of somebody who enhances our own sense of life through her earthy existence. What a wonderful contrast she makes to the portrait of the Parson which follows.

The Parson (479–530)

The portraits of the Parson and the Ploughman should be seen as complementary. Chaucer himself describes them as brothers. This may be a blood relationship but, more likely, Chaucer is referring to brotherhood in Christ, for, while the Parson is a perfect example of the true churchman, the Ploughman is the true secular Christian, obedient and charitable.

One of the great strengths of the *General Prologue* is the way in which Chaucer's ideal characters are convincing. He can make us smile indulgently at such rogues as the Friar or the Wife of Bath, he can make us smile in a slightly superior way at such people as the Merchant and the Guildsmen. He always impresses us when his love of professional skill is expressed in such characters as the Yeoman or the Sergeant of the Law. But with four characters – the Knight, the Clerk, the Parson and the Ploughman – Chaucer gives us an impression of human dignity that is utterly convincing.

All these men, we feel, are mature and experienced. None of them is glamorous or ostentatious. Each is content with his place in the world and is a hard, honest and faithful worker. Each lives by ideals: all four share the ideals of Christianity and the Knight, in addition, lives by the ideals of chivalry. From these qualities stems their concern for other people: the Knight's gentlemanly consideration, the Clerk's willingness to teach and learn, the Ploughman's charity, the Parson's concern to minister to his flock and set a good example.

In the Parson's case, his sense of vocation is placed in complete contrast to that of the other ecclesiastics. Chaucer presents him as poor, learned and utterly sincere. He is also energetic, hard-working and patient. His concern for other people is strenuous and he criticizes the stubborn or hard-hearted sharply and on the spot. His business is the all-important one of saving souls and his vocation is all-absorbing. He visits every one of his parishioners in his wide parish and lets nothing stand in the way of this duty. Above all, he knows that he must set a good example. He practises what he preaches: charity, clean living, moral vigilance. The Parson is oblivious to the various temptations of high office that the Church puts in the path of her ministers: pomp and ceremony, wealth, the easy life and a dulled conscience. The Parson is tempted by none of these. He is too busy getting on with his work.

Such a strong sense of duty and morality is tempered by charity. Again, there is nothing weak about this. The Parson is reluctant to threaten excommunication if his tithes are not paid (though this does not mean that he wouldn't) and, since his parishioners are all poor, he would much rather give of his own small wealth than take from them. Indeed, it is his love for them, his concern for their well-being, that is the guiding force of his life. It is this that prevents him succumbing to the easy life or getting out of touch with their real needs by playing the great churchman. Concern for their welfare ensures that he sets them an example.

The portrait of the Parson again shows Chaucer's reverence for people who live with a sense of responsibility and idealism, who are natural, hard-working and, above all perhaps, loving. The Parson's job is saving souls. No work could be more important or, in this case, better done.

The Ploughman (531–543)

Not every Christian is called to be a man of the Church. The portrait of the Ploughman (a small farmer and not a simple labourer) is a picture of the ideal life of the ordinary man out in the world. He again is an honest worker and a man whose ideals are solid and unpretentious. He lives by Christ's commandments. He loves God and his neighbour as himself, regardless of circumstances. He is a man of charity doing what he can for others for the love of Christ. Furthermore, he is a loyal, honest supporter of the Church.

The portrait is a brief one, but the impression it conveys is again of a contented man at peace with the world: an honest, industrious Christian.

The Miller (547–568)

The portrait of the Miller is a wonderful caricature He is a low, physical, noisy man. Notice how Chaucer concentrates on bodily description to suggest all this. We are shown a prize fighter, rather splendid in his way, but the sort of oaf who can heave a door off its hinges or break it by running at it with his head. An unlikely detail, no doubt, but how well it suggests the sheer unthinking strength of this man. It is like a moment out of a cartoon film. So too are some of the further physical details Chaucer provides: the red beard, the hairs on the wart on his nose and his huge mouth.

We also learn that the Miller is something of a crook – one of his skills is taking three times his allowance of corn. He is a teller of loud and bawdy jokes. Altogether a gross man, but, with his usual refusal to condemn people out of hand, Chaucer tells us that the Miller has a thumb of gold (in other words, he is honest as Millers go), while the pleasing detail of his white coat and blue hood and the picture of him escorting all the pilgrims out of London to the sound of his bagpipes serve to redeem him in our eyes. For all his vulgarity, he is not a bad man. And, of course, he has a part to play in the pilgrimage like everyone else.

The Manciple (569–588)

The Manciple is another example of a pilgrim who is defined entirely by his job. We learn not a single physical detail about him. Instead, Chaucer tells us of his skills. The Manciple was employed to buy provisions for a college or, as here, one of the Inns of Court. Chaucer's

Manciple is exceptionally good at this. Whether he buys in cash or on credit, he always has money in hand.

Nearly half of the lines devoted to him actually describe the managerial skills of the men he looks after. There are a dozen among them well able to supervise the vast estates of the major nobility or the business of a whole shire. The Manciple, in his kind, is actually much more skilful than they are. He is not learned like them and yet he is far more proficient. Such an irony Chaucer attributes to the grace of God who scatters his gifts in a way that is not always obvious.

The Reeve (589–624)

Here is another member of the managerial classes. The Reeve is the person who looked after the estates of a nobleman. Chaucer's Reeve is a particularly severe and forbidding man. We learn that he has a choleric temperament (see pp. 29–30). His closely cropped hair is a sign of his servile station, but his shaved beard and tonsured head suggest a calculating and joyless personality, while his riding at the tail-end of the pilgrims furthers the idea of his suspicious nature. We learn later that the Reeve is the enemy of the Miller, whom we should see as riding near the front of the procession with his bagpipes. The physical contrast between these two is also marked: the Miller is muscular, extrovert and noisy while the Reeve is thin, joyless and suspicious. Both, as it happens, have a good eye for their own profit.

The Reeve's suspicious nature means that he knows exactly what is happening on his lord's estate. The dishonesties of those below him are something he knows all about and, as a result, such people are frightened to death of him. He is, needless to say, superbly efficient. He has complete command of the estate and has had since its owner was twenty. Chaucer provides an impressive list of the things the Reeve has to look after and tells us how he has to supply accounts for these. No one has ever caught him out in this.

In addition, the Reeve looks after himself carefully. A man in a servile position, he has nonetheless amassed quite a lot of money for himself and has the use of a house pleasantly shaded by trees. Indeed, so calculating is he that he can even lend his master the man's own money, earn his thanks and be duly rewarded.

We learn the strange detail – which suggests, perhaps, that this is a portrait taken from life – that the Reeve had once been trained as a carpenter. Nonetheless, the Reeve, as Chaucer presents him, remains the perfect type of the all-efficient, sour and suspicious manager: a person who, while not above dishonesty himself, makes it his business to detect dishonesty in others. What is particularly interesting about this portrait is that it depicts the self-obsession and lack of charity which are the exact opposite of the qualities that Chaucer most admired.

The Summoner (625–670)

The Summoner and his companion, the Pardoner, are among the most memorable of the pilgrims.

The Summoner was the officer who brought people before the courts which, at this period, the Church ran under its own laws. He is a figure at once gross and comically endearing. As with others of his low-lived characters, Chaucer offers a vividly physical description of him which is really a sort of cartoon.

The skin disease that the Summoner is suffering from is a form of leprosy. It disfigures him hideously. Chaucer tells us of the white spots and boils that protrude from his cheeks. The rest of the skin on his face is brilliant red and this is compared (ironically) to the faces of cherubim that were usually painted red at this time. But the Summoner is no angel. He has the narrow eyes of a lecher, and, furthermore, scabby brows and a thin beard. Nothing, it seems, will improve matters. No conventional treatments for skin complaints have any effect at all. In addition, we learn of his taste for blood-heating garlic, onions and leeks and discover that he is a drunk. It is not surprising that children are frightened to look at him.

The Summoner's drunkenness goes with his hot-blooded energy and, as all drinkers were conventionally supposed to, he speaks in Latin when drunk. Not that he knows very much of this: the language of the Church and learned men. Indeed, the few tags of phrases that he does know are things he recites like a tamed bird. Perhaps he cannot even translate them.

But if he is hideous to look at and rather absurd, the Summoner is also corrupt. He lets scoundrels like himself keep their mistresses for a whole year and then lets them off being prosecuted – provided they bribe him with a quart of wine. If this is not too serious a matter, Chaucer takes a far more worried view of things when the Summoner begins to undermine the foundations of the Church's authority: its right to damn souls or save them. In the Summoner's world of bribery and corruption, he takes a wholly cynical view of excommunication (the Church's right to ban people from taking the sacraments), claiming that punishment is only a matter of being fined and otherwise of no consequence. It is certainly nothing to be frightened of. Chaucer wholly disagrees. We have seen that he was aware of abuses in the Church. Most intelligent, sensitive men were. We have seen, too, that he might have agreed with the Monk's criticism of the monastic life. However, Chaucer was not prepared to criticize the true nature and the power of the Church. He strongly disagrees with the Summoner's jibes at the Church's ability to excommunicate and says it is a power men should truly fear. To be denied the right to enter Heaven because one is not allowed to partake in the sacraments of the Church was a very serious matter indeed.

It is important to appreciate this, for the moral corruption of the Summoner is one of the few human frailties pictured in the *General Prologue* which Chaucer is prepared to rebuke sharply. Further, given that his picture of the Summoner shows the man to be immoral, then his friendship with the teenagers in his diocese becomes all the more worrying. Here is a lecherous and energetic drunk with a cynical and ignorant view of the Church who, nonetheless, has all the local young people in his power. He listens to their gossip and gives them advice. This is surely not a healthy state of affairs.

And yet, in the end, Chaucer is never prepared to condemn him out of hand, and the vivid comic details with which he rounds off his portrait of the Summoner go some way to making him appear a more human character than we might have supposed. In the end, we smile at his ridiculous garland and shield made out of a cake or loaf of bread.

The Pardoner (671–716)

Of all the Canterbury pilgrims, the Pardoner is perhaps the strangest. We have seen in many of the preceding portraits that Chaucer had a whole-hearted reverence for the Church and, at the same time, a healthy contempt for its abuses. We have seen too that, when appropriate, he can suggest the low moral standing of his characters through vivid and cartoon-like exaggeration of detail. All these traits combine in the portrait of the Pardoner.

The Pardoner's job was to sell indulgences, the certificates from the Pope which, bought for a certain fee, ensured that a man's sins were forgiven. Christ had given St Peter – and hence the Popes who are believed to be his spiritual descendants – the right not only to forgive sins but to remit the punishments of the afterlife. The true doctrine of the forgiveness of sins relies on full confession, the acceptance of punishment and the devout intention to avoid sin in the future. It requires, in other words, a true moral effort on the part of the sinner. We have seen that the Friar recognizes that some men are too hard-hearted for this. He claims that in such cases the payment of a fine proved such a person was indeed repentant. The pardons (or papal indulgences) that the Pardoner sells rely exclusively on this idea of cash. Like the Summoner, he believes that a man is most effectively punished in his pocket and so he sells forgiveness at a fixed price. In other words, he peddles spiritual values. Such a procedure clearly undermines the true moral authority of the Church.

A further practice open to abuse was the veneration of relics, the belief that piety before the physical remains of a saintly person is a particularly effective form of prayer. This belief, of course, underlies the whole idea of pilgrimage. Chaucer's pilgrims are going to Canterbury so that they can pray at the shrine of the murdered Thomas à Becket. Such efforts may indeed concentrate the mind on the mysteries of the Christian faith. Nonetheless, they are open to abuse and nothing shows this more clearly than the Pardoner touring the country with a pillow-slip that he says is the veil of the Blessed Virgin Mary, the bit of canvas that supposedly comes from the sail of St Peter's boat, and the stones and pigs' bones which are so base that Chaucer refrains from telling us what they were supposed to represent.

Such rampant dishonesty is nothing more than a confidence trick – making money out of the credulity of the ignorant. And making money, of course, is what the Pardoner's business is all about. He is very good at it. The trade in pardons was no doubt a lucrative one and we are told explicitly that the Pardoner himself can make more money in a single day than a poor priest (like the one on the pilgrimage) can in two months. Even in church itself the Pardoner sings and preaches so sweetly that the congregation are all the keener to pay up.

The Pardoner is an utterly reprehensible creature. Chaucer skilfully suggests his moral weakness through his physical ugliness and absurdities. The Pardoner wants to present himself as sexually attractive. He fails lamentably. We could perhaps consider him as an inversion of the Squire. Where that young man is virile, obedient and honest, the thin, streaky, yellow hair of the Pardoner, his staring eyes, feeble voice and hairless chin suggest just the opposite. Chaucer even hints that he may be impotent. Physical impotence, of course, would suit very well with the moral impotence of the Pardoner's trade. His pathetic desires make the Pardoner a dedicated follower of fashion. He refuses to wear his hood and has adopted a new style of riding. All this appears absurd. Yet, despite his worldliness, his physical and moral tawdriness, his sheer sharp practice, Chaucer does not wholly condemn him. The Pardoner may be given over to the wrong things, he may abuse the religious life disgracefully, but 'to tellen, atte laste' as Chaucer says, he is 'a noble ecclesiaste'. This is not simply a sly comment. The Pardoner may indeed be a good churchman for all the wrong reasons (because he wants to make money) but there is no question that the skills he lavishes on his business, especially in church, do indeed enhance other people's faith. The Pardoner has to work hard to get his money, he has to polish his skills – and we have seen that no one admired fine skills more than Chaucer. But, while the Pardoner may be doing this to line his own pockets, he can only effectively do so if the faith of the congregation is genuinely stirred. Dreadful though he is, physically distasteful and morally reprehensible, the Pardoner is finally in the fold of the Church.

The Host – Harry Bailey (749–843)

Harry Bailey is the perfect example of the London landlord: large, extrovert, shrewd and competent. He is genially domineering and has an eye constantly open to profit. He is the perfect man to draw the pilgrims together and lead such a various group.

We are told from the start that his tavern is excellently run and, at the close of the *General Prologue*, Chaucer fills out the portrait of him. We are told how the pilgrims are excellently fed and given fine wine to drink and that their host is large, bright-eyed, forthright and manly. Chaucer tells us that he would have made an excellent major-domo.

His sociable nature comes over (once the pilgrims have paid their bills) when he tells them how pleased he is to see them all and begins to unfold his plan. Notice how his long and rather convoluted speech builds up anticipation and a sense of pleasure and purpose. When Harry Bailey wants to sell an idea he knows just how to do it. The company of pilgrims – and it contains some very forceful and lively characters – is mesmerized by him. Of course, they agree to all he says. It is he who suggests the idea of story-telling, sets out the rules and suggests he be appointed judge and umpire. There is no gainsaying a man like this. Notice, too, how the whole performance is designed to increase his business. The returning pilgrims will all come back to the Tabard where they will pay for the supper of the teller of the best tale.

What we are presented with is thus a man of overflowing vitality and manliness. He is a natural leader, shrewd and perhaps rather domineering, but there is about him that sheer love of life, of bustling, shared human existence, that is immensely invigorating. Harry Bailey is as shrewd and professional as any of the others. He is also as money conscious as most of them. But, like all those Chaucer most admires, Harry Bailey is lively, sociable and well-meaning. He is also perceptive and respectful. His appearance at the end of the *General Prologue* and our last sight of him there as he organizes the lottery to find out who will tell the first story adds immeasurably to the drama, to the happy, trusting, communal excitement of the pilgrimage itself.

The *General Prologue* to the *Canterbury Tales*

Whan that Aprille with his shoures sote
The droghte of Marche hath perced to the rote,
And bathed every veyne in swich licour,
Of which vertu engendred is the flour;
Whan Zephirus eek with his swete breeth
Inspired hath in every holt and heeth
The tendre croppes, and the yonge sonne
Hath in the Ram his halfe cours y-ronne,

(This is intended as a version of the General Prologue *to guide your reading of the original. It is an aid to study and is not intended to stand as a translation in its own right.)*

When April's balmy showers have pierced the dryness of March to its very roots and bathed the veins of each plant with this liquor whose strength gives birth to the flowers; when Zephirus' sweet breath has inspired life in the delicate buds on every wood and heath; when the young sun has run its half-course in the sign of Aries, and the little

Aprille with his shoures sote: The month of April is personified. As a result, the 'sweet showers' seem to fall as if April himself was intent on bringing the world back to life.

perced to the rote: Chaucer emphasizes how completely the showers set about their task. They pierce to the real and metaphorical roots. Compare the phrase: 'to get to the root of the matter'.

vertu engendred: 'Virtue' is the life-force, potency. Its reappearance leads to a literal flowering of nature and, as we shall see, to a metaphorical 'reflowering' of love and life in man. Note the meaning here: it is the flower that is 'engendred' from 'vertu' and not the reborn life-force that is the 'flower' of the process.

Zephirus: Just as April is personified, so is the West wind, which is here given its Latin name. The world of spring is full of benevolent personifications.

the yonge sonne ... y-ronne: We are dealing with the astrological calendar here. The sun was thought to enter Aries (the Ram) on 12 March. The sun was reckoned to stay in this sign until 11 April. It then moved on to Taurus. So, during the month of April, the sun has to finish its time – it's 'half course' – in Aries and then (after 11 April) move on to Taurus. Chaucer tells us that the sun has already run its time in Aries and so the date of the start of the pilgrimage must be after 11 April. Later in the Canterbury Tales the date 18 April is explicitly mentioned.

And smale fowles maken melodye,
That slepen al the night with open yë,   10
(So priketh hem nature in hir corages):
Than longen folk to goon on pilgrimages
(And palmers for to seken straunge strondes)
To ferne halwes, couthe in sondry londes;
And specially, from every shires ende
Of Engelond, to Caunterbury they wende,
The holy blisful martir for to seke,
That hem hath holpen, whan that they were seke.

birds who barely sleep all night sing melodies (because Nature excites their instincts so), then everyone longs to make a pilgrimage. Palmers want to seek out foreign shores and go to distant shrines known of in various lands, while, in particular, from the ends of every shire in England, people journey to Canterbury to seek the holy martyr now in bliss who helped them when they were ill.

slepen al the night with open yë: The birds are said to sleep with their eyes open. In other words, they are so excited they hardly sleep at all. Compare them to the Squire.

So priketh hem . . . : Nature so stimulates their hearts.

palmers ... sondry londes: Spring also awakens religious love (for pilgrimages see p. 10–11, 142). Palmers are, in particular, pilgrims to the Holy Land. Such men seek out foreign shores and distant shrines known in various lands. Palmers returned with the palm branch that gave them their name.

The holy blisful martir: Thomas à Becket was murdered in Canterbury cathedral in 1170. It was soon claimed that his remains worked miracles and his shrine was the most popular goal for pilgrims in England during the Middle Ages. Some pilgrims went to offer thanks for benefits already received (cf. l.18).

    Bifel that, in that seson on a day,
In Southwerk at the Tabard as I lay   20
Redy to wenden on my pilgrimage
To Caunterbury with ful devout corage,
At night was come in-to that hostelrye
Wel nyne and twenty in a companye,
Of sondry folk, by aventure y-falle
In felawshipe, and pilgrims were they alle,
That toward Caunterbury wolden ryde;
The chambres and the stables weren wyde,
And wel we weren esed atte beste.
And shortly, whan the sonne was to reste,   30
So hadde I spoken with hem everichon,
That I was of hir felawshipe anon,
And made forward erly for to ryse,
To take our wey, ther as I yow devyse.

Once it happened at this time of the year that, while I was at the Tabard in Southwark, intending, with devout heart, to go on my own Canterbury pilgrimage, a mixed company of twenty-nine people who happened to have fallen in company came to the inn towards evening. All of them were pilgrims who intended to ride to Canterbury. The rooms and stables were large and we were looked after in the best possible manner. In brief, by the time the sun had set, I had spoken with every one of them and, as a result, had become part of their company and promised to rise early and go with them where I told you we were bound.

Southwerk: the district in London just south of London Bridge. Here is a first example of Chaucer's vivid, concrete detail.

with ful devout corage: Chaucer is a genuine pilgrim.

nyne and twenty: In fact, with attendants, Chaucer and Harry Bailey, there are thirty-two pilgrims.

by aventure y-falle: The idea of chance adds to the realism. In fact, Chaucer the poet has chosen his characters very carefully.

whan the sonne was to reste: in the evening.

made forward: agreed. Chaucer presents himself here as quite a sociable man. Later, he is shown as a rather shy man.

ther as I yow devyse: to the place I told you of, i.e. Canterbury.

But natheles, whyl I have tyme and space,
Er that I ferther in this tale pace,
Me thinketh it acordaunt to resoun,
To telle yow al the condicioun
Of ech of hem, so as it semed me,
And whiche they weren, and of what degree;   40
And eek in what array that they were inne:
And at a knight than wol I first biginne.
  A KNIGHT ther was, and that a worthy man,
That fro the tyme that he first bigan
To ryden out, he loved chivalrye,
Trouthe and honour, fredom and curteisye.
Ful worthy was he in his lordes werre,
And therto hadde he riden (no man ferre)
As wel in Cristendom as hethenesse,
And ever honoured for his worthinesse.   50

Nonetheless, while I have the opportunity, and before I get any further in this matter, it seems to me proper to tell you what each of them was like – at least, how they appeared to me – what they did, what their social standing was, and also what they were wearing. I will start with the Knight.

There was a Knight, a worthy man, who, from the time he first rode out on military exploits, loved chivalry, integrity and honour, liberality and courteous behaviour. He had conducted himself in a praiseworthy manner in his master's wars and in these he had ridden as far as any man, both in Christian and in heathen lands. He had always been honoured for his worthiness.

Me thinketh ... resoun: It seems to me to be in accordance with reason, i.e. reasonable or sensible.

al the condicioun ... hem: As the following lines make clear, Chaucer will describe both the pilgrims' social status and the clothes they wear. But the fascination and greatness of his portraits lie in the realism with which he presents the pilgrims as people.

what degree: their social status. The order of medieval society was different from our own (see pp. 8–9, 132).

ryden out: go off on military expeditions.

chivalrye, Trouthe and honour, fredom and curteisye: These are the knightly values: love of military exploits, integrity, honourable behaviour, liberality and courteous (courtly) manners.

his lordes werre: in the King's service, but also God's.

no man ferre: no man further.

Cristendom ... hethenesse: This is the medieval division of the world into Christian and heathen countries.

At Alisaundre he was, whan it was wonne;
Ful ofte tyme he hadde the bord bigonne
Aboven alle naciouns in Pruce.
In Lettow hadde he reysed and in Ruce,
No Cristen man so ofte of his degree.
In Gernade at the sege eek hadde he be
Of Algezir, and riden in Belmarye.
At Lyeys was he, and at Satalye,
Whan they were wonne; and in the Grete See
At many a noble armee hadde he be.   60
At mortal batailles hadde he been fiftene,
And foughten for our feith at Tramissene
In listes thryes, and ay slayn his foo.
This ilke worthy knight had been also
Somtyme with the lord of Palatye,
Ageyn another hethen in Turkye:

He was at Alexandria when it was taken. He had often been awarded the place of honour at the high table in Prussia above men from other nations. He had been on expeditions in Lithuania and Russia more frequently than any Christian of his status. He had also been at Granada during the siege of Algeciras, and had been in service in the kingdom of Ben-marin. He was at Ayas and Attalia when they were won, and with many noble armies around the Mediterranean. He had been in fifteen mortal combats. He had fought three times in tournaments for the Christian faith at Tlemsen and always slain his foe. This same worthy knight had also on one occasion been with the ruler of Palatia, fighting against more heathens in Turkey.

Alisaundre: Alexandria was won and immediately abandoned in 1365.

the bord bigonne: placed at the head of the table as the guest most to be honoured.

Pruce ... Lettow ... Ruce: Prussia ... Lithuania ... Russia: all places where medieval English knights went to fight when in need of employment.

Gernade ... Algezir: Algeciras (which is near Cape Trafalgar in southern Spain) was taken from the Moorish King of Granada (Gernade) in 1344.

Belmarye ... Lyeys ... Satalye: The first was a Moorish kingdom in Africa, the second was in Armenia and won from the Turks in 1367. Satalye, on the south coast of Asia Minor, was won in 1362.

the Grete See: the Mediterranean.

mortal batailles: fights to the death.

Tramissene: a Moorish kingdom in North Africa. Here the Knight had fought three times, one to one, against a heathen opponent, killing all three contestants.

Palatye: He had, on one occasion (*not* 'sometimes'), fought the Turkish heathens with the Christian overlord of Palatye in Anatolia.

And evermore he hadde a sovereyn prys.
And though that he were worthy, he was wys,
And of his port as meke as is a mayde.
He never yet no vileinye ne sayde   70
In al his lyf, un-to no maner wight.
He was a verray parfit gentil knight.
But for to tellen yow of his array,
His hors were gode, but he was nat gay.
Of fustian he wered a gipoun
Al bismotered with his habergeoun;
For he was late y-come from his viage,
And wente for to doon his pilgrimage.
    With him ther was his sone, a yong SQUYER,
A lovyere, and a lusty bacheler,   80
With lokkes crulle, as they were leyd in presse.
Of twenty yeer of age he was, I gesse.
Of his stature he was of evene lengthe,
And wonderly deliver, and greet of strengthe.

He always won the highest renown and, although he was valiant, he was prudent and behaved as meekly as a young girl. He had never yet said anything unworthy of a gentleman to anyone of any sort whatsoever. He was a truly complete, well-mannered knight. But, to tell you how he was dressed: while his horse was in good condition, he himself was not extravagantly rigged out. He wore a thick cotton surcoat which was dirtied from his chainmail, for he had only recently returned from his journeying and was now going on his pilgrimage.

His son was with him, a young Squire, a lover and a vigorous young knight in the making. The tight locks of his hair looked as if they had been put in curling tongs. I should think he was about twenty years old. He was of average height, wonderfully agile and very strong.

a sovereyn prys: great renown.

though that he were worthy, he was wys: Although he was a man of honour, he was prudent.

He never yet … maner wight: For a discussion of this sentence see p. 14.

parfit: complete, finished.

Of fustian … habergeoun: He wore a tight fitting vest or doublet made of thick cotton which was dirtied from his coat of mail.

his viage: his journeying.

bacheler: a young man hoping to be a knight. 'Bacheler' does not simply mean he was unmarried.

lokkes crulle: The Squire's locks of hair were so curly that they might have been put in curling tongs.

evene lengthe: average height.

deliver: Notice that Chaucer shows the Squire as being neither a mere dandy nor merely crudely physical.

And he had been somtyme in chivachye,
In Flaundres, in Artoys, and Picardye,
And born him wel, as of so litel space,
In hope to stonden in his lady grace.
Embrouded was he, as it were a mede
Al ful of fresshe floures, whyte and rede.   90
Singinge he was, or floytinge, al the day;
He was as fresh as is the month of May.
Short was his goune, with sleves longe and wyde.
Wel coude he sitte on hors, and faire ryde.
He coude songes make and wel endyte,
Iuste and eek daunce, and wel purtreye and wryte.

He had spent some time on military service in Flanders, Artois and Picardy and had conducted himself well, as so short a space of time allowed, in the hope of standing high in his lady's favour. His clothes were embroidered all over so that he looked like a field full of fresh flowers, white and red. He sung or played the flute all day long and was as fresh as the month of May. His short gown had long wide sleeves. He sat well on his horse and rode it excellently. He could compose tunes and write lyrics for them, joust, dance, draw well and write.

Flaundres ... Artoys ... Picardye: So far the young squire has only been on campaigns in France and northern Europe. Compare these to his father's exploits.

In hope to stonden in his lady grace: The Squire is presented as a young courtly lover. He fights to win the 'grace' – in other words the favour – of the woman he loves. He has conducted himself well in the short time he has been fighting.

Embrouded was he ...: The Squire is wearing the short coat with long, wide sleeves that was very fashionable at the time. Chaucer gently pokes fun at the lavish embroidery on it, saying the young man looks like a field full of spring flowers, and describes him as as light-hearted as May.

Singinge ... floytinge: Singing and playing the flute are amongst the Squire's many cultured, courtly activities.

He coude songes make: He could compose tunes.

wel endyte: He could also write good lyrics for them.

Iuste: joust.

wel purtreye and wryte: He could draw well and write. Neither were automatic accomplishments, even among the aristocracy.

So hote he lovede, that by nightertale
He sleep namore than dooth a nightingale.
Curteys he was, lowly, and servisable,
And carf biforn his fader at the table.   100

   A YEMAN hadde he, and servaunts namo
At that tyme, for him liste ryde so;
And he was clad in cote and hood of grene;
A sheef of pecok-arwes brighte and kene
Under his belt he bar ful thriftily;
(Wel coude he dresse his takel yemanly:
His arwes drouped noght with fetheres lowe),
And in his hand he bar a mighty bowe.
A not-heed hadde he, with a broun visage.
Of wode-craft wel coude he al the usage.   110

He was so passionately in love that he didn't sleep at night any more than a nightingale does. He was courteous, humble, willing to serve, and he carved the meat before his father at table.

He had a Yeoman but no other servants with him at that time. It pleased him to ride thus. The Yeoman wore a coat and hood of green. Under his belt he had a sheaf of bright, sharp arrows with peacock-feather flights ready to hand. (He knew very well how to look after his equipment in a yeoman-like way. *His* arrows did not have bedraggled flights.) He carried a mighty bow in his hand. He had closely cropped hair and a tanned face. He knew all the skills of woodland life.

So hote ...: He was so ardently in love that, at night time, he slept no more than a nightingale. The nightingale is the bird of love and in the Middle Ages it was believed not to sleep during the mating season.

Curteys ... at the table: The Squire had the humble manners proper to one of his years and station. He was willing to behave in this way. As his father's chief servant, he performed the duty of carving the meat before him. This was a traditional duty of squires. Chaucer knew about this from personal experience (see p. 11).

A Yeman hadde he: 'He' here refers to the Knight. Both the Squire and the Yeoman act as his servants. At this period (*c*.1400) a yeoman was the title of a servant immediately above a groom. It did not yet mean a small landowner.

dresse his takel: He could look after his equipment (which included arrows with peacock-feather flights) in a way that did proper justice to his station in life. The flights on his arrows were not crushed and bedraggled.

not-heed: closely cropped hair (a sign of servile status).

Of wode-craft: He well understood all the skills of woodland life. There were far more forests in England at that time than now. Late in life Chaucer was appointed to look after the forests of the King.

Upon his arm he bar a gay bracer,
And by his syde a swerd and a bokeler,
And on that other syde a gay daggere,
Harneised wel, and sharp as point of spere;
A Cristofre on his brest of silver shene.
An horn he bar, the bawdrik was of grene;
A forster was he, soothly, as I gesse.

    Ther was also a Nonne, a PRIORESSE,
That of hir smyling was ful simple and coy;
Hir gretteste ooth was but by sëynt Loy;   120
And she was cleped madame Eglentyne.
Ful wel she song the service divyne,

On his arm he wore a bright guard. He had a sword and small shield on one side and on the other a fancy dagger, beautifully fitted out and as sharp as the point of a spear. He wore a shining silver medal of St Christopher. He carried a horn on a green baldric. I am sure he must have been a forester.

There was also a nun – a Prioress – who smiled in a charming and unaffected manner. Her greatest oath was only sworn by St Loy. Her name was Madame Eglentyne. She sang divine service beautifully,

bracer: a protection for the inside of the left forearm against the bow string.

Harneised: equipped, decked out.

Cristofre: He wears a medallion representing St Christopher. It was a good luck charm. Amongst other things, St Christopher was held to protect one against unforeseen accidents. He was also the patron saint of foresters.

bawdrik: a belt that ran over one shoulder and under the opposite arm.

Prioresse: the female head of a small religious house.

simple and coy: modest, charming and unaffected.

sëynt Loy: This was traditionally the mildest of oaths, in other words, no oath at all.

Entuned in hir nose ful semely;
And Frensh she spak ful faire and fetisly,
After the scole of Stratford atte Bowe,
For Frensh of Paris was to hir unknowe.
At mete wel y-taught was she with-alle;
She leet no morsel from hir lippes falle,
Ne wette hir fingres in hir sauce depe.
Wel coude she carie a morsel, and wel kepe,   130
That no drope ne fille up-on hir brest.
In curteisye was set ful muche hir lest.
Hir over lippe wyped she so clene,
That in hir coppe was no ferthing sene
Of grece, whan she dronken hadde hir draughte.
Ful semely after hir mete she raughte,

intoning in her nose in a becoming manner, and she spoke competent, graceful Anglo-French in the accent of the school of Stratford-by-Bow. Parisian French was unknown to her. She had been taught excellent table manners. She didn't let a drop fall from her lips, nor did she dip her fingers too deeply into the sauce. She managed her food in such a way that none of it fell on her breast. Her great pleasure in life was refined behaviour. She wiped her top lip so clean that not the smallest grease stain could be seen on her beaker when she had drunk her measure. She reached for her food in the most seemly way.

Entuned in hir nose: Intoning through the nose was traditional at church services. Perhaps it was meant to avoid straining the throat. Like all her other behaviour, this is very ladylike.

the scole of Stratford atte Bowe: This does *not* mean she spoke French badly. It means she spoke the Anglo-French common to most upper-class English people after the Norman Conquest and therefore she belonged (and made sure others were aware of it) to this social group. Madame Eglentyne had been educated in the English convent of St Leonard at Stratford by Bow in London. This was why she did not know Parisian French. The French she did speak was not necessarily held to be inferior, it merely had a different accent.

Ne wette hir fingres...: Her table manners (in a period before the introduction of the fork) are impeccable. She does not dip her fingers in too deeply, let food drop from her mouth or fall on her clothes. She does not have greasy lips which leave smears on her beaker, nor does she grab after her food.

In curteisye was set ...: Her great pleasure in life was adhering to the forms of etiquette.

And sikerly she was of greet disport,
And ful plesaunt, and amiable of port,
And peyned hir to countrefete chere
Of court, and been estatlich of manere,   140
And to ben holden digne of reverence.
But, for to speken of hir conscience,
She was so charitable and so pitous,
She wolde wepe, if that she sawe a mous
Caught in a trappe, if it were deed or bledde.
Of smale houndes had she, that she fedde
With rosted flesh, or milk and wastel-breed.
But sore weep she if oon of hem were deed,
Or if men smoot it with a yerde smerte:
And al was conscience and tendre herte.   150

And, truly, she was very genial, pleasant and friendly and she made great efforts to imitate the manners of the court and carry herself in a stately way so as to be held worthy of deference. But, to talk of her feelings, she was so kind-hearted and full of pity that she would cry if she saw a dead or bleeding mouse caught in a trap. She had a number of little dogs that she fed on roast meat, milk and the finest white bread. She would weep bitterly if one of them died or if anyone hit it with a rule. Everything with her was refined and tender feeling.

greet disport: full of geniality.

peyned hir . . . : She made great efforts to imitate the manners of the court. What does this fact tell us about a lady supposedly given to the religious life?

estatlich . . . reverence: dignified in bearing and to be thought of as worthy of reverence.

rosted flesh, or milk and wastel-breed: Her little dogs, for which she has great sentimental love, were pampered on roast meat and bread made only from the best flour. Nuns were not supposed to keep dogs at all.

Ful semely hir wimpel pinched was;
Hir nose tretys; hir eyen greye as glas;
Hir mouth ful smal, and ther-to softe and reed;
But sikerly she hadde a fair forheed;
It was almost a spanne brood, I trowe;
For, hardily, she was nat undergrowe.
Ful fetis was hir cloke, as I was war.
Of smal coral aboute hir arm she bar
A peire of bedes, gauded al with grene;
And ther-on heng a broche of gold ful shene,   160
On which ther was first write a crowned A,
And after, *Amor vincit omnia.*

    Another NONNE with hir hadde she,
That was hir chapeleyne, and PREESTES three.

Her wimple was becomingly pleated. She had a long, straight nose, eyes grey as glass and a very small mouth, which was soft and red. She also had a fine forehead that was, I would say, nearly a hand's breadth broad. She herself wasn't short. I noticed that her cloak was very neat. Around her arm she wore a coral rosary, the gauds of which were green. From this hung a shining gold brooch on which was inscribed an A with a crown over it followed by the motto: *Amor vincit omnia* ('Love conquers all').

She had another nun with her, who was her chaplain, and three priests.

Ful semely hir wimpel pinched was: Her wimple – the cloth that covered her neck – was carefully pleated.

tretys: long and well-shaped.

a spanne brood: as wide as the palm of the hand.

nat undergrowe: Note Chaucer's tactful way of saying that the Prioress is a large lady.

A peire of bedes, gauded al with grene: The Prioress wears round her arm a rosary or string of beads which is designed to help prayer. The majority of the beads are small coral ones, but every eleventh bead was larger. These were called 'gaudies'. Here they are covered in green stuff. As the rosary is told, so the 'gaudies' remind the user to say an 'Our Father' or a 'Hail Mary'.

Amor vincit omnia: 'Love conquers all.' The capital 'A' of this motto on the Prioress's brooch has a crown on top of it. The love referred to is divine love. Compare the brooches of the Yeoman and Monk.

hir chapeleyne: The Prioress is attended by three priests, one of whom tells the delightful *Nun's Priest's Tale*. Her 'chaplain' was her secretary and, of course, female.

A MONK ther was, a fair for the maistrye,
An out-rydere, that lovede venerye;
A manly man, to been an abbot able.
Ful many a deyntee hors hadde he in stable:
And, whan he rood, men mighte his brydel here
Ginglen in a whistling wind as clere,   170
And eek as loude as dooth the chapel-belle.
Ther as this lord was keper of the celle,
The reule of seint Maure or of seint Beneit,
By-cause that it was old and som-del streit,
This ilke monk leet olde thinges pace,
And held after the newe world the space.

There was a Monk, a surpassingly fine man, who looked after the outlying properties of his house. He loved hunting and was a virile fellow, fit to be an abbot. He had many fine horses in his stables and, when he rode, you could hear his bridle jingling in a whistling wind as clearly and loudly as a chapel bell. At the place where this lordly man was prior, the rules of St Maur or St Benedict, since they were old-fashioned and rather strict, he let pass by unheeded. He behaved as modern ways dictate.

a fair for the maistrye: excellent, surpassing all others.

out-rydere: one who looks after the outlying properties belonging to a large religious foundation.

manly man . . . able: a fine figure of a man, well up to being an abbot.

Ther as: at the place where.

keper of the celle: prior of a small monastery or dependent religious house.

The reule of seint Maure or of seint Beneit: The strict monastic rules of St Benedict and his disciple St Maur are the oldest forms of discipline in Roman Catholic monastic orders.

By-cause: since, seeing that.

leet olde thinges pace: let old-fashioned ways pass by unheeded.

held after the newe world the space: held his course (i.e. behaved) as modern fashions suggest.

He yaf nat of that text a pulled hen,
That seith, that hunters been nat holy men;
Ne that a monk, when he is recchelees,
Is lykned til a fish that is waterlees;   180
This is to seyn, a monk out of his cloistre.
But thilke text held he nat worth an oistre;
And I seyde, his opinioun was good.
What sholde he studie, and make him-selven wood,
Upon a book in cloistre alwey to poure,
Or swinken with his handes, and laboure,
As Austin bit? How shal the world be served?
Lat Austin have his swink to him reserved.
Therfore he was a pricasour aright;
Grehoundes he hadde, as swifte as fowel in flight;   190
Of priking and of hunting for the hare
Was al his lust, for no cost wolde he spare.
I seigh his sleves purfiled at the hond
With grys, and that the fyneste of a lond;
And, for to festne his hood under his chin,
He hadde of gold y-wroght a curious pin:

He cared nothing for the text that says that hunters are not holy men and that a monk who is carefree is like a fish out of water. He said that piece of wisdom wasn't worth an oyster. And I said he was right. Why should he study and drive himself mad by always poring over some book or other in his cloister, or labouring and working with his hands as St Augustine bade? What good will this do the world? Let Augustine do his labouring for himself! As a result, he was a hard-riding hunter, who had greyhounds swift as flying birds. Riding and hunting hares was, indeed, his whole delight in life and he spared no expense on it. I noticed that his sleeves were trimmed about the wrists with expensive grey fur, the best that can be got. While, to fasten his hood under his chin, he had a finely wrought golden pin

yaf nat of that text a pulled hen: A text here means something often quoted. A 'pulled' or plucked hen is something worthless. A modern colloquial equivalent might be: 'He did not give a fig for it'.

recchelees: careless.

til: to.

a fish that is waterlees: a fish out of water.

wood: mad.

swinken ... Austin bit?: work with his hands and labour as St Augustine bade. Complaints against the worldly, comfortable lives of monks were widespread.

Lat Austin ... reserved: Let St Augustine do his own hard work!

a pricasour aright: a hard-riding hunter or one who tracks a hare by its footprints. The former meaning is probably intended here.

for no cost: for no expense.

purfiled ... With grys: edged with costly grey fur at the wrist. This is another reference to the Monk's worldliness.

A love-knotte in the gretter ende ther was.
His heed was balled, that shoon as any glas,
And eek his face, as he had been anoint.
He was a lord ful fat and in good point;   200
His eyen stepe, and rollinge in his heed,
That stemed as a forneys of a leed;
His botes souple, his hors in greet estat.
Now certeinly he was a fair prelat;
He was nat pale as a for-pyned goost.
A fat swan loved he best of any roost.
His palfrey was as broun as is a berye.
    A FRERE ther was, a wantown and a merye,
A limitour, a ful solempne man.
In alle the ordres foure is noon that can   210

in the broader end of which was a love-knot. His bald head shone like glass, as did his face, which looked as if it had been anointed. He was plump and in excellent physical condition. His eyes rolled round his face which was bright and fiery and shone like the fir under a cauldron. His boots were fine and supple, his horse was in excellent fettle. He was certainly a splendid churchman. He did not look like a suffering ghost. He liked a fat swan best of all roast meats. His horse was as brown as a berry.

There was a Friar, a loose-living and jolly Limiter who enjoyed good living. In all the four orders there is no man who knows

A love-knotte: The Monk wore an elaborate golden brooch with a complicated twist of loops at its wider end. Compare the brooches of the Yeoman and the Prioress.

balled: bald.

as he: as if he.

His eyen ... of a leed: His eyes, that rolled round in his face, were bright and fiery, while his face itself shone like the fire under a cauldron. Note the order of ideas here. It is the eyes that shine like fire, not the face.

for-pyned goost: a tortured, starving ghost.

A limitour: The Friar belonged to a mendicant or begging order and had assigned to him a certain district or 'limit' in which he could beg for alms. This he had to pay a licence fee for.

solempne: The meaning here is probably cheerful or festive rather than pompous.

alle the ordres foure: There were four orders or types of friars. They were known as the Dominicans or Black Friars, the Franciscans or Grey Friars, the Carmelites or White Friars, and the Augustinian Friars.

So muche of daliaunce and fair langage.
He hadde maad ful many a mariage
Of yonge wommen, at his owne cost.
Un-to his ordre he was a noble post.
Ful wel biloved and famulier was he
With frankeleyns over-al in his contree,
And eek with worthy wommen of the toun:
For he had power of confessioun,
As seyde him-self, more than a curat,
For of his ordre he was licentiat.   220
Ful swetely herde he confessioun,
And plesaunt was his absolucioun;
He was an esy man to yeve penaunce
Ther as he wiste to han a good pitaunce;
For unto a povre ordre for to yive
Is signe that a man is wel y-shrive.

so much about gossip and flattery. He had married off a great many young women at his own expense. He was a pillar of his community. He was well-liked and on good terms with wealthy landowners over all his part of the countryside, and also with well-to-do women in the town since he had, as he himself said, more extensive powers of confession than a parish priest for he was a licenciate of his order. He heard confession most indulgently and gave absolution lightly. He ordered an easy penance where he thought he would get a generous reward of food: for giving to an order of poor monks is a sign that a man has made full confession.

daliaunce and fair langage: gossip and flattery. The portrait of the Friar is another attack on the worldliness of the medieval Church.

ful many a mariage ... cost: He had married off many young women at his own expense. This is not necessarily charity on the Friar's part. The women may well have been his mistresses.

frankeleyns: prosperous landowners. Chaucer, of course, includes a portrait of one here (ll. 333–62.

power of confessioun: authority to hear confession and award penance and absolution.

more than a curat ... licentiat: He had a licence from the Pope to hear all confessions. The local priest (or 'curat') could not always grant absolution or forgiveness as the Friar could.

esy man ... pitaunce: He granted absolution easily (i.e. readily and painlessly) when he was sure he would be well rewarded. The payment here was made in food.

y-shrive: forgiven.

For if he yaf, he dorste make avaunt,
He wiste that a man was repentaunt.
For many a man so hard is of his herte,
He may nat wepe al-thogh him sore smerte.   230
Therfore, in stede of weping and preyeres,
Men moot yeve silver to the povre freres.
His tipet was ay farsed ful of knyves
And pinnes, for to yeven faire wyves.
And certeinly he hadde a mery note;
Wel coude he singe and pleyen on a rote.
Of yeddinges he bar utterly the prys.
His nekke whyt was as the flour-de-lys;
Ther-to he strong was as a champioun.
He knew the tavernes wel in every toun,   240
And everich hostiler and tappestere
Bet than a lazar or a beggestere;
For un-to swich a worthy man as he
Acorded nat, as by his facultee,

If a man gave so, this Friar dared boast that he knew the man was truly repentant. Indeed, many people are so hard-hearted that they cannot weep for their sins, although they are sorely grieved by them. Therefore, instead of weeping and prayers, such men should give silver to the poor friars. His loose hood was garnished with knives and pins to give to pretty women. He was certainly very cheerful. He could sing nicely, play the fiddle, and always won the prize hands down for popular romantic songs. His neck was as white as a lily. In addition, he was as strong as a champion wrestler. He knew the public houses, the publicans and barmaids in every town far better than he knew the lepers and beggarwomen, for it was unsuitable, considering his position,

make avaunt: boast.

him sore smerte: his sins pain him deeply. The corruption of the Friar lies partly in his too ready acceptance of money as a sign that a man has repented.

His tipet was ay farsed . . .: The knives that the Friar carried in his hood were love-gifts for local women. Women wore small sheaved knives at their girdles. They were often marriage gifts.

yeddinges: popular songs telling a tale. These are another sign of the Friar's worldliness and his ability to earn cash and rewards.

tappestere: female publican. These were more common in the Middle Ages than now.

lazar or a beggestere: Leprosy was widespread. Such a disease usually entailed begging for a living. 'Beggestere' is a female beggar.

Acorded nat, as by his facultee: It was unsuitable, considering his ability or position. Yet another sign of the Friar's wordliness getting the better of Christian charity.

To have with seke lazars aqueyntaunce.
It is nat honest, it may nat avaunce
For to delen with no swich poraille,
But al with riche and sellers of vitaille.
And over-al, ther as profit sholde aryse,
Curteys he was, and lowly of servyse.   250
Ther nas no man no-wher so vertuous.
He was the beste beggere in his hous;
And yaf a certeyn ferme for the graunt;
Noon of his bretheren cam ther in his haunt;
For thogh a widwe hadde noght a sho,
So plesaunt was his '*In principio*',
Yet wolde he have a ferthing, er he wente.
His purchas was wel bettre than his rente.
And rage he coude, as it were right a whelpe.
In love-dayes ther coude he muchel helpe.   260
For there he was nat lyk a cloisterer,
With a thredbar cope, as is a povre scoler,
But he was lyk a maister or a pope.
Of double worsted was his semi-cope,
That rounded as a belle out of the presse.

to have acquaintance with the leperous. It is not honest, nor does it do a man any good, to have dealings with such low people, but only to mix with the rich and with sellers of food. Above all, he was courteous and servile where he knew he could get money. No man anywhere was so virtuous. He was the best beggar in his religious house, and gave an annual payment to be licensed to beg. This kept his fellow friars off his patch. Even if a widow had not a penny to her name, so ingratiating was his *In principio* that he would get a farthing from her before he left. The proceeds of his begging in this way were far greater than his income from other sources. He could romp about as if he were a puppy. He was of great assistance at Love-days, for he was not like a poor scholar, bound to his cloister and dressed in threadbare clothes, but like a senior churchman or even a pope. His short cloak was made of thick worsted material and was as fully rounded as a bell just out of the mould.

poraille: the rabble of poor people.

ther as profit sholde aryse: Profit is the Friar's chief motive.

And yaf . . . haunt: He gave an annual payment to be licensed to beg, which kept his fellow friars off his patch. Another example of his commercialism.

'*In principio*': 'In the beginning', the opening of St John's gospel, a favourite text.

His purchas . . . . rente: The proceeds of his begging in this way ('purchas' implies gains wrongfully won) were greater than his income from other sources. 'Rente' does *not* refer to what he paid to secure rights over his territory.

love-dayes: days when private disputes were settled by an umpire without going to court. Churchmen were usually employed as the umpires. It was another way of enriching themselves.

Somwhat he lipsed, for his wantownesse,
To make his English swete up-on his tonge;
And in his harping, whan that he had songe,
His eyen twinkled in his heed aright,
As doon the sterres in the frosty night.   270
This worthy limitour was cleped Huberd.

   A MARCHANT was ther with a forked berd,
In mottelee, and hye on horse he sat,
Up-on his heed a Flaundrish bever hat;
His botes clasped faire and fetisly.
His resons he spak ful solempnely,
Souninge alway thencrees of his winning.
He wolde the see were kept for any thing
Bitwixe Middelburgh and Orewelle.
Wel coude he in eschaunge sheeldes selle.   280
This worthy man ful wel his wit bisette;
Ther wiste no wight that he was in dette,
So estatly was he of his governaunce,
With his bargaynes, and with his chevisaunce.
For sothe he was a worthy man with-alle,
But sooth to seyn, I noot how men him calle.

By way of affectation he lisped a little to make his English sweeter on the tongue. When he was playing the harp and had sung his song, his eyes twinkled in his head like the stars in the frosty night. This worthy Limiter was called Hubert.

There was a Merchant with a forked beard. Dressed in a coat of rich, mixed material, he sat upright on his horse. There was a Flemish beaver hat on his head and his boots were nice and neatly buckled. He gave his opinion pompously, always hinting at his making more money. He wished that, regardless of cost, the sea between Middleburgh and Harwich were kept free of pirates. He knew very well how to sell French crowns for a profit on the money markets. This good man was so shrewd, so dignified in his bearing when he bargained and made agreements to borrow money, that no one realized he was in debt. Surely he was a fine man, but, to be honest, I don't know what his name was.

forked berd: a beard branching out to two points. These were fashionable in the Middle Ages. Some illuminated manuscripts show Chaucer with such a beard.

ful solempnely ... his winning: The Merchant is rather pompous and boring about his single-minded pursuit of money.

He wolde the see ... Orewelle: He wanted the sea to be kept clear of pirates, regardless of the cost. The stretch of sea which the Merchant's ships ply is between Middleburgh in Holland and Harwich, by the estuaries of the rivers Stour and Orwell.

in eschaunge sheeldes selle: He sold French crowns for profit on the money markets. Such forms of currency dealing were illegal.

So estatly ... chevisaunce: He bore himself in such a stately way when bargaining and agreeing to borrow money – and he also employed his knowledge to such advantage – that no one realized he was in debt.

I noot how men him calle: Chaucer does not know his name. This is sometimes read as the sneer of a courtly poet at the merchant classes.

A CLERK ther was of Oxenford also,
That un-to logik hadde longe y-go.
As lene was his hors as is a rake,
And he nas nat right fat, I undertake;   290
But loked holwe, and ther-to soberly.
Ful thredbar was his overest courtepy;
For he had geten him yet no benefyce,
Ne was so worldly for to have offyce.
For him was lever have at his beddes heed
Twenty bokes, clad in blak or reed,
Of Aristotle and his philosophye,
Than robes riche, or fithele, or gay sautrye.
But al be that he was a philosophre,
Yet hadde he but litel gold in cofre;   300
But al that he mighte of his freendes hente,
On bokes and on lerninge he it spente,

There was an Oxford Clerk, too. He had long given himself over to the study of logic. His horse was as thin as a rake and, I can tell you, he wasn't very fat either, but looked serious and hollow-cheeked. His short outer cloak was threadbare for he had not yet got himself a position in the Church and was not worldly enough to have a secular post. He would rather have twenty volumes of Aristotle and his philosophy bound in black and red at his bed's head than rich clothes, fiddles and psalteries. Nonetheless, although he was a philosopher, he had little gold to his name. Rather, all he could obtain from his friends was spent on books and learning

Clerk: a university student, a scholar, a man of learning or one in holy orders. This Clerk is an example of the 'perpetual student'.

y-go: given himself.

benefyce ... to have offyce: He had not got himself a paid job in the Church and was too unworldly to get secular employment. Many clerks got jobs in the law or administration because they were able to read and write.

Twenty bokes ... philosophye: Twenty is a round number but suggests a large private library for the time. This is how the Clerk spent – or would have liked to spend – his money. Aristotle was the Greek philosopher whose teaching underlay much medieval thought.

But al be that he ... cofre: Chaucer is making a pun. He is referring to the alchemists, scholars whose search for the 'philosopher's stone' which would turn everything to gold, beggered them. Like them, the Clerk has failed to make much money.

al that he mighte ... hente: In a time before grants for study, poor scholars were required to beg or borrow for their studies.

And bisily gan for the soules preye
Of hem that yaf him wher-with to scoleye.
Of studie took he most cure and most hede.
Noght o word spak he more than was nede,
And that was seyd in forme and reverence,
And short and quik, and ful of hy sentence.
Souninge in moral vertu was his speche,
And gladly wolde he lerne, and gladly teche.   310

   A SERGEANT OF THE LAWE, war and wys,
That often hadde been at the parvys,
Ther was also, ful riche of excellence.
Discreet he was, and of greet reverence:
He semed swich, his wordes weren so wyse.
Iustyce he was ful often in assyse,
By patente, and by pleyn commissioun;
For his science, and for his heigh renoun
Of fees and robes hadde he many oon.
So greet a purchasour was no-wher noon.   320
Al was fee simple to him in effect,
His purchasing mighte nat been infect.

while he set himself to pray earnestly for the souls of those who gave him the wherewithal to study. Study, indeed, was his overriding interest. He didn't speak one word more than was necessary and what he said was said properly, modestly, pithily and in a learned manner. His words were full of moral virtue. He would gladly learn and gladly teach.

There was also a Sergeant of the Law, cautious and shrewd, who had often attended the Parvis. He was an excellent man: discreet, learned – at least he seemed so, his words were so wise. He had often been an assize judge both as an appointee and by letters patent. Because of his knowledge and reputation, he had earned many fees and payments in kind. Nowhere was there so great a purchaser of land. Virtually everything was his freehold. There were no ties to what he bought.

forme and reverence ... hy sentence: in a dignified, terse and well-informed manner.

A Sergeant of the Lawe: a barrister of more than sixteen years' standing and one of the King's legal servants.

parvys: There is some dispute as to whether this was the porch of St Paul's, a court at Westminster or a mock trial among students at the Inns of Court. Whichever, the line suggests that the Sergeant of the Law was a well-known, senior figure.

Iustyce ... pleyn commissioun: He had acted as a judge both from appointment made by the King's letter patent and (prior to this) on a less permanent basis when an appointee. Both appointments gave him jurisdiction over all kinds of cases.

fees and robes: He had been paid both in cash and in clothes.

purchasour ... fee simple: He bought up large areas of land. He always bought freeholds so that the land was his and his heirs' for ever.

No-wher so bisy a man as he ther nas,
And yet he semed bisier than he was.
In termes hadde he caas and domes alle,
That from the tyme of king William were falle.
Therto he coude endyte, and make a thing,
Ther coude no wight pinche at his wryting;
And every statut coude he pleyn by rote.
He rood but hoomly in a medlee cote   330
Girt with a ceint of silk, with barres smale;
Of his array telle I no lenger tale.
      A FRANKELEYN was in his companye;
Whyt was his berd, as is the dayesye.
Of his complexioun he was sangwyn.
Wel loved he by the morwe a sop in wyn.
To liven in delyt was ever his wone,
For he was Epicurus owne sone,
That heeld opinioun, that pleyn delyt
Was verraily felicitee parfyt.   340
An housholdere, and that a greet, was he;
Seint Iulian he was in his contree.

Nowhere was there a busier man, yet he seemed busier than he actually was. He knew how to express in the proper terms all the legal cases and decisions that had been ruled in the courts since the time of William the Conqueror. Moreover, he could dictate and draft an agreement such that no one could cavil at what he wrote. And he knew every statute off by heart. He rode in a homely way in a coat of rich, mixed stuff which was held in by a band of silk with narrow stripes of colour on it. I'll say no more about what he wore.

The Franklin was his companion. His beard was as white as a daisy and his complexion was sanguine. He liked his piece of cake or bread dipped in wine of a morning. His custom was to live a life of pleasure. He was a true son of Epicurus and believed that unadulterated delight is the most perfect form of content. He ran a considerable household and was the St Julian of his area.

In termes ... were falle: He knew how to express in the proper terms all the legal cases and decisions that had been ruled in the courts since the time of William the Conqueror, i.e. for nearly three hundred years.

every statut ...: He knew all the common law by heart.

Frankeleyn: a considerable landowner not of noble birth.

Of his complexioun he was sangwyn: A person's 'complexion' is his or her temperament. This, in turn, was dependent on the four 'humours' (hot, cold, moist and dry), which were thought to make up everything (see pp. 29–30). In the sanguine or contented temperament, the hot and moist humours predominated.

Epicurus: Greek philosopher who held that pleasure was the highest good.

Seint Iulian: patron saint of hospitality and comfort.

His breed, his ale, was alwey after oon;
A bettre envyned man was no-wher noon.
With-oute bake mete was never his hous,
Of fish and flesh, and that so plentevous,
It snewed in his hous of mete and drinke,
Of alle deyntees that men coude thinke.
After the sondry sesons of the yeer,
So chaunged he his mete and his soper.   350
Ful many a fat partrich hadde he in mewe,
And many a breem and many a luce in stewe.
Wo was his cook, but-if his sauce were
Poynaunt and sharp, and redy al his gere.
His table dormant in his halle alway
Stood redy covered al the longe day.
At sessiouns ther was he lord and sire;
Ful ofte tyme he was knight of the shire.
An anlas and a gipser al of silk
Heng at his girdel, whyt as morne milk.   360
A shirreve hadde he been, and a countour;
Was no-wher such a worthy vavasour.

His bread and ale were always of the same highest quality and no man had a better wine cellar. His house was never without baked meat, fish and other flesh, and those in such great quantities that his house seemed to snow down meat, drink and all the good things a man can think of. He changed his meals and diet according to the various seasons of the year. There were many fat partridges in his mews and shoals of bream and pike in his stew ponds. His cook was in severe trouble if ever his sauces weren't sharp or his utensils ready to hand. His dining-table stood ready and covered in his hall all day. He had been a Justice of the Peace and a Member of Parliament on many occasions. A short two-edged sword and a silk purse, white as morning milk, hung from his girdle. He had been Sheriff and County Auditor Nowhere was there such a worthy landowner.

alwey after oon: uniformly high standard.

envyned: stored with wine.

After: according to.

mewe: mew, a place for fattening birds for the table.

stewe: stew pond, a pond for fattening fish for the table.

table dormant: a permanent dining-table. These were new in Chaucer's period and suggested great hospitality.

At sessiouns ... knight of the shire: The Franklin took his duties seriously. He was both a Justice of the Peace and a Member of Parliament. Chaucer was the latter briefly during 1387.

A shirreve ... and a countour: He had also been Sheriff or governor of his county. A 'countour' probably refers to his having been auditor or accountant to his shire.

vavasour: One who holds his land not directly from the King, but indirectly through one of the King's vassals. In other words, he was the vassal of a vassal. But he was not a servant.

An HABERDASSHER and a CARPENTER,
A WEBBE, a DYERE, and a TAPICER,
Were with us eek, clothed in o liveree,
Of a solempne and greet fraternitee.
Ful fresh and newe hir gere apyked was;
Hir knyves were y-chaped noght with bras,
But al with silver, wroght ful clene and weel,
Hir girdles and hir pouches every-deel.   370
Wel semed ech of hem a fair burgeys,
To sitten in a yeldhalle on a deys.
Everich, for the wisdom that he can,
Was shaply for to been an alderman.
For catel hadde they y-nogh and rente,
And eek hir wyves wolde it wel assente;
And elles certein were they to blame.
It is ful fair to been y-clept '*ma dame*',

A Haberdasher, and a Carpenter, a Weaver, a Dyer and an Upholsterer were also with us. They were all clothed in the livery of a great and solemn brotherhood. Their possessions were new and spruce. Their knives were not capped with brass but with silver. Their belts and pouches were cleanly and beautifully made. Each of them seemed a citizen fine enough to sit with the governors at the high table. Each of them, considering his expertise, was worthy of being the alderman of his guild. Each had enough property and income for this, and besides their wives were very keen on the idea and would have thought themselves blameworthy otherwise. It is very nice to be called 'Madam'

An Haberdassher and a Carpenter, A Webbe, a Dyere and a Tapicer: These five are, respectively: a seller of sewing materials or hats, a carpenter, a male weaver, a dyer of cloth and an upholsterer. They are wealthy tradespeople.

greet fraternitee: Since they all belong to different guilds, their 'fraternity' must be a religious or social group whose uniform or livery they are wearing. One might compare this to a modern Rotary Club.

Hir knyves ... with silver: Their silver-decorated knives are a sign of their social status. Poorer people would not have been able to afford such finery.

a fair burgeys ... on a deys: prosperous citizens worthy of sitting with the aldermen at the high table.

For catel ... and rente: For each of them had sufficient property and income to be an alderman or head of the guild. Note the different meaning of the word 'rent'.

hir wyves ... to blame: Note the order of ideas: it was the wives who would have thought themselves deserving of blame if their husbands were not promoted to the position of alderman. In other words, the wives were snobs.

And goon to vigilyës al bifore,
And have a mantel royalliche y-bore.   380
   A COOK they hadde with hem for the nones,
To boille the chiknes with the mary-bones,
And poudre-marchant tart, and galingale.
Wel coude he knowe a draughte of London ale.
He coulde roste, and sethe, and broille, and frye,
Maken mortreux, and wel bake a pye.
But greet harm was it, as it thoughte me,
That on his shine a mormal hadde he;
For blankmanger, that made he with the beste.
   A SHIPMAN was ther, woning fer by weste: 390
For aught I woot, he was of Dertemouthe.
He rood up-on a rouncy, as he couthe,
In a gowne of falding to the knee.
A daggere hanging on a laas hadde he
Aboute his nekke under his arm adoun.
The hote somer had maad his hewe al broun;
And, certeinly, he was a good felawe.
Ful many a draughte of wyn had he y-drawe
From Burdeux-ward, whyl that the chapman sleep.
Of nyce conscience took he no keep.   400

and take the front place at vigils and have your mantle carried like a queen.

They had brought a Cook with them for the occasion to boil chickens with marrow bones and sharp flavouring powder and sweet cyperus root. He was a connoisseur of London ale. He knew how to roast, seethe, broil and fry, make mortreux and bake good pies. But I thought it was a great pity that he had a growth on his shin. He made white meat dishes with the best of them.

There was a Shipman who lived in the far West Country. For all I know he came from Dartmouth. He rode an old nag as best he could and wore a knee-length gown of coarse cloth. A dagger hung from a strap that went round his neck and down under his arm. He was very sun-tanned from the hot summer and he was quite a rogue. He had stolen, while he sailed the Bordeaux route, a great deal of wine while the merchant who owned it was asleep. He was not troubled with a delicate conscience.

to vigilyës al bifore: The snobbery of the wives is re-emphasized. They enjoyed being called 'Madam' at guild feasts prior to guild festivals or 'vigils' and being the 'top' people there.

for the nones: for the occasion.

mortreux: The pronunciation of this word is uncertain. It was a soup made either from chicken, pork, breadcrumbs, egg yolks and saffron or fish roes and liver, bread, pepper and ale.

woning: living.

rouncy: an old nag. The Shipman is not comfortable on a horse.

good felawe: a fairly light-hearted hint that he is a bit of a rogue.

whyl that the chapman sleep: He stole the wine from the sleeping merchant who had hired his ship to transport the wine from Bordeaux.

nyce: refined.

If that he faught, and hadde the hyer hond,
By water he sente hem hoom to every lond.
But of his craft to rekene wel his tydes,
His stremes and his daungers him bisydes,
His herberwe and his mone, his lodemenage,
Ther nas noon swich from Hulle to Cartage.
Hardy he was, and wys to undertake;
With many a tempest hadde his berd been shake.
He knew wel alle the havenes, as they were,
From Gootlond to the cape of Finistere,   410
And every cryke in Britayne and in Spayne;
His barge y-cleped was the Maudelayne.

    With us ther was a DOCTOUR OF PHISYK,
In al this world ne was ther noon him lyk
To speke of phisik and of surgerye;
For he was grounded in astronomye.
He kepte his pacient a ful greet del
In houres, by his magik naturel.

If he had to fight and got the upper hand then he made his enemies 'walk the plank'. But, as to his skill, in reckoning tides, currents, the risks of sailing, harbours, the position of the moon and the piloting of a boat, there was no one like him from Hull to Cartagena. He was tough and experienced. His beard had been shaken by many a tempest. He knew by heart all the inlets from Gottland to Cape Finistere and every creek in Brittany and Spain. His boat was called the *Magdalene*.

There was a Physician with us. In matters of medicine and surgery there was none in the world to equal him, for he was trained in astronomy. He kept his patients alive for many hours through natural magic.

By water . . .: He made them 'walk the plank'. Or, maybe, he just pitched them overboard.

his tydes: Note Chaucer's delight in the Shipman's technical terms and skills.

Hardy he was . . .: sufficiently tough and experienced.

grounded in astronomye: trained in astronomy or, more properly, astrology. Before the development of scientific medicine, healing was much involved with astrological ideas, as the following lines show (see pp. 29–31).

a ful greet del In houres: These are the astrological hours. The exact position of the heavenly bodies, their 'aspects' or 'ascendant' were important for the effect of the talismans the Doctor made of the signs of the Zodiac (see l. 418). (It is possible that the talisman was a wax figure of the patient.)

magik naturel: 'Natural magic' was regarded as a legitimate science while 'black magic', of course, was not.

Wel coude he fortunen the ascendent
Of his images for his pacient.   420
He knew the cause of everich maladye,
Were it of hoot or cold, or moiste, or drye,
And where engendred, and of what humour;
He was a verrey parfit practisour.
The cause y-knowe, and of his harm the rote,
Anon he yaf the seke man his bote.
Ful redy hadde he his apothecaries,
To sende him drogges and his letuaries,
For ech of hem made other for to winne;
Hir frendschipe nas nat newe to biginne.   430
Wel knew he the olde Esculapius,
And Deiscorides, and eek Rufus,
Old Ypocras, Haly, and Galien;
Serapion, Razis, and Avicen;
Averrois, Damascien, and Constantyn;
Bernard, and Gatesden, and Gilbertyn.

He knew perfectly how to foretell the beneficial aspects of the astrological talismans he had made for his patients. He knew the cause of every sickness, whether it originated in the hot, cold, moist or dry humours, from what part of the body the disturbance issued and which humour was responsible for it. He was a completely knowledgeable practitioner. Having once diagnosed the root and cause of the patient's illness, he gave the sick man the right remedy. He had his apothecaries to hand to send him drugs and medicines. He and they worked to their mutual advantage. They had known each other for a long time. He was well read in the ancient works of Aesculapius, Dioscorides, Rufus, old Hippocrates, Alhazen, Galen, Serapion, Rhazes, Avicenna, Averroes, Damascien, Constantinus Afer, Bernard Gordon, John Gatesden and Gilbertus Anglicus.

hoot ... humour: The four elementary qualities of hot, cold, moist and dry, it was believed, made up all things. Illness was thought to be caused by an imbalance in these. The mixture of these 'humours' determined a man's complexion or temperament (see notes to ll. 335 and 589, and pp. 29–30).

yaf the seke man his bote: gave him his remedy.

apothecaries: makers–up of drugs. These were men less qualified than doctors and held in low regard, being sometimes considered dishonest and in league with the doctors at the patient's expense. See next note.

ech of hem ... to biginne: This idea of the doctors and apothecaries joining to fleece the patient is here made explicit. The two are old allies.

Esculapius ... Gilbertyn: Chaucer here parades his own learning with a list of eminent authorities dating from Aesculapius, the legendary father of Greek medicine, through later Greek, Roman, Arab and modern authorities.

Of his diete mesurable was he,
For it was of no superfluitee,
But of greet norissing and digestible.
His studie was but litel on the Bible.   440
In sangwin and in pers he clad was al,
Lyned with taffata and with sendal;
And yet he was but esy of dispence;
He kepte that he wan in pestilence.
For gold in phisik is a cordial,
Therfore he lovede gold in special.
   A good WYF was ther of bisyde BATHE,
But she was som-del deef, and that was scathe.
Of clooth-making she hadde swiche an haunt,
She passed hem of Ypres and of Gaunt.   450
In al the parisshe wyf ne was ther noon
That to the offring bifore hir sholde goon;
And if ther dide, certeyn, so wrooth was she,
That she was out of alle charitee.
Hir coverchiefs ful fyne were of ground;
I dorste swere they weyeden ten pound
That on a Sonday were upon hir heed.
Hir hosen weren of fyn scarlet reed,
Ful streite y-teyd, and shoos ful moiste and newe.
Bold was hir face, and fair, and reed of hewe.   460

He was moderate in his diet and what he ate, rather than being excessive, was nourishing and easily digested. He rarely read the Bible. He was dressed in blood-red cloth and bluish-grey fur lined with taffeta and fine silk. Yet he was careful with his money and saved what he earned in times of plague. Since gold is a tonic in medicine, he loved gold particularly.

There was a fine Wife from the neighbourhood of Bath, though it was a shame that she was somewhat deaf. She was so skilled in making cloth that she surpassed the weavers of Ypres and Ghent. No woman in the whole parish was to precede her to the offertory and, if one did, there was no question but that she was so angry that she lost all charitable feelings. The headscarves that she wore were of the finest material, and I daresay those that were on her head on Sundays weighed ten pounds. Her tightly gartered stockings were bright red and her shoes were supple and fashionable. She had a bold, attractive and ruddy face.

His studie . . . on the Bible: Doctors were commonly thought of as being sceptics or even atheists. They were believed to be more interested in experiments than in God.

In sangwin . . . : The Doctor's clothes betray the money he has made.

gold in phisik is a cordial: Gold was supposed to be a very effective medicine, but the implication here is that the Doctor does better from it than the patient.

Ypres and of Gaunt: These were the great cloth markets of Europe. The cloth makers of the West Country were famous for their quality.

offring: The congregation offered the priests bread and wine as gifts on these occasions, which gave rise to many arguments as to who had the right to go before others.

She was a worthy womman al hir lyve,
Housbondes at chirche-dore she hadde fyve,
Withouten other companye in youthe;
But therof nedeth nat to speke as nouthe.
And thryes hadde she been at Ierusalem;
She hadde passed many a straunge streem;
At Rome she hadde been, and at Boloigne,
In Galice at seint Iame, and at Coloigne.
She coude muche of wandring by the weye.
Gat-tothed was she, soothly for to seye.   470
Up-on an amblere esily she sat,
Y-wimpled wel, and on hir heed an hat
As brood as is a bokeler or a targe;
A foot-mantel aboute hir hipes large,
And on hir feet a paire of spores sharpe.
In felawschip wel coude she laughe and carpe.
Of remedyes of love she knew per-chaunce,
For she coude of that art the olde daunce.

She had been a fine-looking woman all her life. She had married five times, besides what company she had known in her young days – but there is no need to speak of that now. She had been to Jerusalem three times and crossed many foreign rivers. She had been to Rome, Boulogne-sur-mer, the shrine of St James in Compostella and to Cologne. She knew a great deal about wandering one way and another. To tell the truth, her teeth were set widely apart. She rode an ambling horse in a comfortable way, wearing many wimples, a hat as wide as a shield or buckler and a riding-habit over her generous hips. There were a pair of sharp spurs on her feet. She laughed and jested in company. Maybe she knew about love-potions, for she knew all the old tricks of that game.

at chirche-dore: The celebration of marriage at the door of the church was usual until the sixteenth century. A nuptial mass was then celebrated at the altar.

other companye: her lovers before she was married.

Ierusalem . . . Coloigne: The Wife of Bath had been on many pilgrimages before. Her motives, as she tells in the *Prologue* to her own Tale, were not always of the highest. Pilgrimages offered a fairly safe form of travel at a difficult and dangerous time. They were also a way of meeting people away from home. The shrine of St James at Compostella in Spain was the most famous in medieval Europe.

She coude . . . by the weye: She knew much about travel but also, it is suggested, about veering off the straight and narrow.

Gat-tothed: supposedly a sign of a traveller. In her tale the Wife of Bath associates her widely spaced teeth with her amorous nature.

foot-mantel: This kept her warm and protected. She was riding side-saddle.

the olde daunce: the old game.

A good man was ther of religioun,
And was a povre PERSOUN of a toun;   480
But riche he was of holy thoght and werk.
He was also a lerned man, a clerk,
That Cristes gospel trewely wolde preche;
His parisshens devoutly wolde he teche.
Benigne he was, and wonder diligent,
And in adversitee ful pacient;
And swich he was y-preved ofte sythes.
Ful looth were him to cursen for his tythes,
But rather wolde he yeven, out of doute,
Un-to his povre parisshens aboute   490
Of his offring, and eek of his substaunce.
He coude in litel thing han suffisaunce.
Wyd was his parisshe, and houses fer a-sonder,
But he ne lafte nat, for reyn ne thonder,
In siknes nor in meschief, to visyte
The ferreste in his parisshe, muche and lyte,
Up-on his feet, and in his hand a staf.
This noble ensample to his sheep he yaf,
That first he wroghte, and afterward he taughte;
Out of the gospel he tho wordes caughte;   500
And this figure he added eek ther-to,
That if gold ruste, what shal iren do?
For if a preest be foul, on whom we truste,
No wonder is a lewed man to ruste;

There was a good churchman, a poor town parson who was, none-theless, rich in holy thoughts and deeds. Moreover, he was a learned man, able to read and write, and one who preached the gospel of Christ honestly and taught his parishioners devoutly. He was kindly, extremely diligent and patient in adversity, as had often been shown. He was loathe to excommunicate a person for not paying their tithes. There is no doubt that he would rather give his poor parishioners a share of what he received at the offering or from his own pocket. A little sufficed him. His parish was extensive, the houses were far apart, but, despite rain, thunder, sickness or trouble he never failed to visit even the most distant of his parishioners – both rich and poor – on foot and with his staff in his hand. He set his flock this fine example: he first practised what he preached. He took his text from the Bible and added this illustration to it: 'If gold rusts, what will happen to iron?' For, if a priest whom we trust lives badly, it is small wonder that an uneducated person should be corrupted.

Cristes gospel . . . preche: This is a great contrast to all the other church-men we have met so far; so too is his behaviour. Here is a rare glimpse of a humble, honest ecclesiastic.

tythes: Tithes were the tax of one tenth of a man's income levied by the Church. Failure to pay could result in excommunication – the withdrawal of the right to take part in the sacraments of the Church.

offring: see note to l.452.

sheep: i.e. his parishioners.

figure: figure of speech.

gold ruste . . .: The ideal priest is a golden example. Pure gold is incorruptible.

And shame it is, if a preest take keep,
A shiten shepherde and a clene sheep.
Wel oghte a preest ensample for to yive,
By his clennesse, how that his sheep shold live.
He sette nat his benefice to hyre,
And leet his sheep encombred in the myre,   510
And ran to London, un-to sëynt Poules,
To seken him a chaunterie for soules,
Or with a bretherhed to been withholde;
But dwelte at hoom, and kepte wel his folde,
So that the wolf ne made it nat miscarie;
He was a shepherde and no mercenarie.
And though he holy were, and vertuous,
He was to sinful man nat despitous,
Ne of his speche daungerous ne digne,
But in his teching discreet and benigne.   520
To drawen folk to heven by fairnesse
By good ensample, was his bisinesse:
But it were any persone obstinat,
What-so he were, of heigh or lowe estat,
Him wolde he snibben sharply for the nones.
A bettre preest, I trowe that nowher noon is.
He wayted after no pompe and reverence,
Ne maked him a spyced conscience,
But Cristes lore, and his apostles twelve,
He taughte, and first he folwed it him-selve.   530

A mindful priest would see that it is a disgrace to have a filthy shepherd but clean sheep. A priest should set an example by his own clean life of how his flock should live. He didn't hire out his parish and leave his sheep straggling in the filth, while he went off to St Paul's to seek out a chantry chapel or to be kept in retirement by a brotherhood. He stayed at home and looked after his flock to see that the wolf did them no harm. He was a true shepherd, not a hireling. Nonetheless, although he was a virtuous and holy man, he was neither contemptuous towards sinful men nor unapproachable and scornful of speech, rather was his teaching kindly and thoughtful. His concern was to draw people to Heaven by a good life and setting a good example. However, if anyone were obstinately sinful, whoever he was, high or low, he would sharply reprove him there and then. I believe there is no better priest anywhere. He didn't hanker after pomp and being reverenced, nor did he cultivate an over-subtle conscience, rather he taught the teachings of Christ and the twelve Apostles – but he followed them himself first.

A shiten shepherde ...: The priest is the shepherd of his flock. He should be cleaner than his sheep.

benefice ... bretherhed: He did not appoint a curate to do the hard work while he ran off to London to earn an easy second living by praying for the soul of a rich man in a chantry chapel (a small chapel built for this purpose) or by retreating into a wealthy religious order.

wolf: the enemy of the sheep (or parishioners), who were in the care of the shepherd (or parson).

mercenarie: a hireling shepherd, considered untrustworthy.

snibben sharply: Although humble and kindly, the Parson is no moral coward and speaks up for what is right. Compare him to the Friar.

wayted after ... spyced conscience: The Parson is neither overbearing nor hypocritical and over-refined in matters of conscience.

With him ther was a PLOWMAN, was his brother,
That hadde y-lad of dong ful many a fother,
A trewe swinker and a good was he,
Livinge in pees and parfit charitee.
God loved he best with al his hole herte
At alle tymes, thogh him gamed or smerte,
And thanne his neighebour right as him-selve.
He wolde thresshe, and ther-to dyke and delve,
For Cristes sake, for every povre wight,
Withouten hyre, if it lay in his might.   540
His tythes payed he ful faire and wel,
Bothe of his propre swink and his catel.
In a tabard he rood upon a mere.

   There was also a Reve and a Millere,
A Somnour and a Pardoner also,
A Maunciple, and my-self; ther were namo.

   The MILLER was a stout carl, for the nones,
Ful big he was of braun, and eek of bones;
That proved wel, for over-al ther he cam,
At wrastling he wolde have alwey the ram.   550
He was short-sholdred, brood, a thikke knarre,
Ther nas no dore that he nolde heve of harre,
Or breke it, at a renning, with his heed.
His berd as any sowe or fox was reed,
And ther-to brood, as though it were a spade.

His brother, the Ploughman, accompanied him. He had carted many a load of dung in his time. He was a true and honest worker, living in peace and perfect charity. He loved God best with his whole heart and at all times, good or bad, and then he loved his neighbour as himself. Whenever he could he would thresh and dig and excavate ditches for every poor soul without charge and for the love of Christ. He paid his tithes fully and punctually both on his labour and his property. He wore a ploughman's smock and rode on a mare.

There was also a Reeve, a Miller, a Summoner, a Pardoner, a Manciple and myself – there were no others.

The Miller was a burly fellow, brawny and big-boned, which was shown by his always winning the ram over all-comers at wrestling matches. He was short-shouldered and thick-set, and there was no door that he couldn't heave off its hinges or smash by running at it with his head. His beard was as red as the bristles of any pig or fox and as broad as a spade.

Plowman . . . brother: The Ploughman is a poor farmer and *not* a mere labourer. He may actually be the Parson's brother as well as, in Christian terms, his spiritual brother, though the latter meaning is the more likely.

He wolde thresshe: He would work free for others as a true act of Christian charity. This is something most of the churchmen would not do.

His tythes . . . catel: He paid his church taxes in full both on the fruits of his own labour and on his property.

mere: a horse for poor people.

the ram: This was the traditional prize at wrestling matches which the Miller's great strength means he always wins.

Up-on the cop right of his nose he hade
A werte, and ther-on stood a tuft of heres,
Reed as the bristles of a sowes eres;
His nose-thirles blake were and wyde.
A swerd and bokeler bar he by his syde;   560
His mouth as greet was as a greet forneys.
He was a Ianglere and a goliardeys,
And that was most of sinne and harlotryes.
Wel coude he stelen corn, and tollen thryes;
And yet he hadde a thombe of gold, pardee.
A whyt cote and a blew hood wered he.
A baggepype wel coude he blowe and sowne,
And ther-with-al he broghte us out of towne.

    A gentil MAUNCIPLE was ther of a temple,
Of which achatours mighte take exemple   570
For to be wyse in bying of vitaille.
For whether that he payde, or took by taille,
Algate he wayted so in his achat,
That he was ay biforn and in good stat.

He had a wart on the right side of the tip of his nose and on this there stood a tuft of hairs as red as the bristles in a sow's ears. His nostrils were black and wide. He carried a sword and buckler by his side. His mouth was as gaping as a great furnace. He was a loud talker and a teller of bawdy jokes. He was adept at stealing corn and trebling the toll he was allowed to take, and yet, to be sure, he had a thumb of gold. He wore a white coat and a blue hood. He was a skilful bagpipe player and to the sound of this he accompanied us out of town.

There was a charming Manciple from one of the Inns of Court, whom all such purchasers might take as an example of how to be skilled in buying food; for, whether he paid cash or took his goods on credit, he always timed his purchases so that he had money in hand.

Ianglere and a goliardeys: a loud and foul-mouthed man.

stelen corn, and tollen thryes: Millers (who were traditionally regarded as dishonest, as Chaucer makes plain in the *Reeve's Tale*) were allowed a proportion of what they ground in addition to a fee. This Miller took three times what he was allowed.

a thombe of gold: He was honest as far as millers go. It was a proverbial expression that an honest miller had a thumb of gold.

Maunciple: the man responsible for provisioning a college or, as here, an Inn of Court, which was a centre for barristers (as we call them now).

temple: one of the Inns of Court.

took by taille: The tally is a wooden stick on which notches recorded goods bought on credit.

ay biforn . . .: He always secured excellent bargains and so had money in hand.

Now is nat that of God a ful fair grace,
That swich a lewed mannes wit shall pace
The wisdom of an heep of lerned men?
Of maistres hadde he mo than thryes ten,
That were of lawe expert and curious;
Of which ther were a doseyn in that hous,   580
Worthy to been stiwardes of rente and lond
Of any lord that is in Engelond,
To make him live by his propre good,
In honour dettelees, but he were wood,
Or live as scarsly as him list desire;
And able for to helpen al a shire
In any cas that mighte falle or happe;
And yit this maunciple sette hir aller cappe.

    The REVE was a sclendre colerik man,
His berd was shave as ny as ever he can.   590
His heer was by his eres round y-shorn.
His top was dokked lyk a preest biforn.
Ful longe were his legges, and ful lene,
Y-lyk a staf, ther was no calf y-sene.
Wel coude he kepe a gerner and a binne;
Ther was noon auditour coude on him winne.

Now, isn't that a wonderful example of God's grace that the skills of an unlettered man such as he should outpace the wisdom of a mass of educated men? He looked after more than thirty masters, professional men, who were expert and learned in the law and of whom a dozen in the establishment were qualified to be stewards of the income and lands of any lord in England, and so allow him either to live off his own funds and honourably clear of debt (unless he were mad) or as frugally as he might wish. They could also have administered an entire county, despite anything that might happen. Nonetheless, this Manciple out-capped them all.

The Reeve was a slender, choleric man. His beard was as closely shaved as is possible, his hair was cropped about his ears and he was tonsured like a priest. His legs were long and thin, like a stick. You could see no calves on them at all. He knew exactly how to look after a granary and a wheat bin so that no auditor could catch him out.

maistres: professional men, masters of an art.

propre good: own funds.

helpen al a shire: look after the affairs of a whole county.

sette hir aller cappe: outcapped them all, i.e. was smarter than them all.

Reve: A Reeve is the manager of a large estate.

a sclendre colerik man: The choleric or quick-tempered complexion was the result of a predominance of the hot and dry humours. For an explanation of the theory see notes to ll. 335 and 422 and pp. 29–30.

His heer ...: His close-cropped hair was a sign of his servile status. Compare the Yeoman.

auditour: The accounts of the estate were checked by an outside man.

Wel wiste he, by the droghte, and by the reyn,
The yelding of his seed, and of his greyn.
His lordes sheep, his neet, his dayerye,
His swyn, his hors, his stoor, and his pultrye,   600
Was hoolly in this reves governing,
And by his covenaunt yaf the rekening,
Sin that his lord was twenty yeer of age;
Ther coude no man bringe him in arrerage.
Ther nas baillif, ne herde, ne other hyne,
That he ne knew his sleighte and his covyne;
They were adrad of him, as of the deeth.
His woning was ful fair up-on an heeth,
With grene treës shadwed was his place.
He coude bettre than his lord purchace.   610
Ful riche he was astored prively,
His lord wel coude he plesen subtilly,
To yeve and lene him of his owne good,
And have a thank, and yet a cote and hood.
In youthe he lerned hadde a good mister;
He was a wel good wrighte, a carpenter.
This reve sat up-on a ful good stot,
That was al pomely grey, and highte Scot.

He knew from whether it had been a wet or a dry season what the yield of seed and grain would be. In addition, his lord's sheep, cattle, dairy, swine, horses, stores and poultry were completely in the Reeve's management and, by agreement, he had supplied the account for these ever since his master was twenty years old. No man could prove him in default. There was no bailiff, herdsman or other labourer whose sharp practices and deceits he wasn't aware of. They were scared to death of him. His house was pleasantly situated on a heath and shaded by green trees. He could make purchases far more shrewdly than his master. He had secretly amassed himself considerable wealth and knew how to please his lord subtly by giving and lending him of that lord's own money and yet still earn his thanks and a coat and a hood. In his youth he had learned a good trade and had been an excellent carpenter. He rode on a fine dappled grey cob called Scot.

covenaunt: legal agreement.

covyne: This is a deceitful agreement between two parties to cheat a third.

His woning ... : The Reeve has managed to get a very pleasant house for himself.

he was astored prively: He hid his considerable gains well.

His lord ... cote and hood: He could lend his master his own money back without the master realizing it, and earn a coat and hood as a grateful reward. This is a vivid example of the Reeve's business ability.

mister: a 'mystery' or skilled trade.

A long surcote of pers up-on he hade,
And by his syde he bar a rusty blade.   620
Of Northfolk was this reve, of which I telle,
Bisyde a toun men clepen Baldeswelle.
Tukked he was, as is a frere, aboute,
And ever he rood the hindreste of our route.

   A SOMNOUR was ther with us in that place,
That hadde a fyr-reed cherubinnes face,
For sawcefleem he was, with eyen narwe.
As hoot he was, and lecherous, as a sparwe;
With scalled browes blake, and piled berd;
Of his visage children were aferd.   630
Ther nas quik-silver, litarge, ne brimstoon,
Boras, ceruce, ne oille of tartre noon,
Ne oynement that wolde clense and byte,
That him mighte helpen of his whelkes whyte,
Nor of the knobbes sittinge on his chekes.
Wel loved he garleek, oynons, and eek lekes,
And for to drinken strong wyn, reed as blood.
Thanne wolde he speke, and crye as he were wood.

He wore a long, blue-grey overcoat and carried a rusty sword at his side. This Reeve I am describing came from near a town called Baldswell in Norfolk. He wore his coat tucked into his girdle like a friar and he always rode at the rear of our company.

There was a Summoner with us. He had the fiery red face of a cherubim for he was afflicted with pimply skin and he had narrow-set eyes. He was as hot-blooded and lecherous as a sparrow and had scabby black eyebrows and a scanty beard. Children were frightened by his face. There was no mercury, white-lead, sulphur, borax, leaden salve or cream of tartar, nor any other ointment that cleanses or cauterizes, that could in any way help him get rid of the white pimples and knobs that perched on his cheeks. He loved garlic, onions and leeks and was partial to red wine that was as strong as blood. Under its influence he would talk and cry out like a mad man.

And ever he rood ... : While this shows the Reeve's naturally secretive nature, it is also a position he takes up for his own safety. He and the Miller are deadly enemies and it is the Miller with his bagpipes who rides at the front of the pilgrims and leads them out along the road. These two will later tell tales at the expense of each other's skills.

Somnour: the officer who brought accused people before an ecclesiastical court.

a fyr-reed cherubinnes face: Cherubs were conventionally painted with red faces.

sawcefleem: having a red, pimpled face.

eyen narwe ... sparwe: a sign of a lustful nature. Sparrows were conventionally considered lecherous.

quik-silver ... byte: conventional remedies for clearing the skin. The Summoner's complaint was so bad that none of them worked.

garleek, oynons, and eek lekes: These were all held to heat the blood.

And whan that he wel dronken hadde the wyn,
Than wolde he speke no word but Latyn.   640
A fewe termes hadde he, two or three,
That he had lerned out of som decree;
No wonder is, he herde it al the day;
And eek ye knowen wel, how that a Iay
Can clepen 'Watte', as well as can the pope.
But who-so coude in other thing him grope,
Thanne hadde he spent al his philosophye;
Ay '*Questio quid iuris*' wolde he crye.
He was a gentil harlot and a kinde;
A bettre felawe sholde men noght finde.   650
He wolde suffre, for a quart of wyn,
A good felawe to have his concubyn
A twelf-month, and excuse him atte fulle:
Ful prively a finch eek coude he pulle.
And if he fond o-wher a good felawe,
He wolde techen him to have non awe,
In swich cas, of the erchedeknes curs,
But-if a mannes soule were in his purs;

When he had drunk a good deal of wine, then he would speak only Latin. He knew two or three legal phrases that he had learned out of some decree or other, which is scarcely to be wondered at since he heard them being used all day, and you know how even a tamed jay can call 'Walter' as well as the Pope himself can. However, if anyone tested him any further, then his learning was exhausted. 'What is the law that applies here?' he would exclaim. He was a gentle, kindly rascal and you'd never find a better rogue anywhere. Given a quart of wine, he would allow any scoundrel to keep his mistress for a year and then fully excuse him for it. He knew how to secretly wring the unwary dry. And, if he found a kindred spirit anywhere, he would tell him not to be frightened of the archdeacon's powers of excommunication unless he thought his soul resided in his purse,

And whan ... Latyn: It was a proverb that drunk men spoke Latin. The more drunk they got, the more supposedly intricate the Latin became.

a Iay Can clepen 'Watte': literally Wat or Walter. In other words, like a tamed bird he could 'speak' but did not know what the words meant.

'Questo quid iuris': 'What part of the law applies here?' The phrase, which was common in legal matters, means nothing to the drunken Summoner.

Ful prively ... pulle: He knew how to get the feathers (i.e. money) off a bird (i.e. an inexperienced person).

the erchedeknes curs: The archdeacon, a churchman of moderate standing, had the right to excommunicate sinners, i.e. refuse them the sacraments (see pp. 36–7, 138–9).

But-if ... purs: unless a man believed his soul lived in his purse. An empty purse was all the 'Hell' the archdeacon could sentence a man to.

For in his purs he sholde y-punisshed be.
'Purs is the erchedeknes helle,' seyde he.   660
But wel I woot he lyed right in dede;
Of cursing oghte ech gilty man him drede –
For curs wol slee, right as assoilling saveth –
And also war him of a *significavit*.
In daunger hadde he at his owne gyse
The yonge girles of the diocyse,
And knew hir counseil, and was al hir reed.
A gerland hadde he set up-on his heed,
As greet as it were for an ale-stake;
A bokeler hadde he maad him of a cake.   670
    With him ther rood a gentil PARDONER
Of Rouncival, his freend and his compeer,
That streight was comen fro the court of Rome.
Ful loude he song, 'Com hider, love, to me'.
This somnour bar to him a stif burdoun,
Was never trompe of half so greet a soun.

for it was in his purse that he would be punished. 'The purse is where the archdeacon's hell is to be found,' he said. But I knew he was lying. Every guilty man should be afraid of excommunication for it means eternal death, just as absolution means saving for eternal life. A man should also be wary of a *significavit*. The Summoner had within his control and in his own way all the young people of the diocese and he knew their secrets and gave them advice. He wore on his forehead a garland big enough to be an inn-sign and he had made himself a shield from a loaf of bread.

A pleasant Pardoner attached to the foundation of the Blessed Mary of Roncesvalles, the Summoner's close friend, rode with him. He had just come from the papal court at Rome. He sang loudly, 'Come hither, love, to me!' The Summoner sang the refrain in the bass part – no trumpet was ever half so loud.

curs wol slee ...: Chaucer is at pains to disagree with the Summoner. The guilty should fear excommunication since it leads to damnation as surely as absolution saves a man.

significavit: the opening words of the writ remanding an excommunicated person to prison.

In daunger ... al hir reed: He had within his control (and at his mercy) all the young people of the diocese. He was privy to their secrets and advised them. Was his interest wholly good?

Pardoner Of Rouncival: Pardoners sold papal indulgences, the certificates of the forgiveness of sins that were bought at a high price. Such things, as we have seen (p. 38), were a disgraceful racket. Pardoners did not have to be in holy orders. The 'Rouncival' referred to is the foundation of the Blessed Mary of Roncesvalles at Charing Cross. The original Ronceval is in France. The Pardoner had been to Rome rather than there.

'*Com hider, love, to me*': This is a line of a popular song.

a stif burdoun: This is the refrain of the song (or 'carol') which is sung in the bass line.

This pardoner hadde heer as yelow as wex,
But smothe it heng, as dooth a strike of flex;
By ounces henge his lokkes that he hadde,
And ther-with he his shuldres overspradde;   680
But thinne it lay, by colpons oon and oon;
But hood, for Iolitee, ne wered he noon,
For it was trussed up in his walet.
Him thoughte, he rood al of the newe Iet;
Dischevele, save his cappe, he rood al bare.
Swiche glaringe eyen hadde he as an hare.
A vernicle hadde he sowed on his cappe.
His walet lay biforn him in his lappe,
Bret-ful of pardoun come from Rome al hoot.
A voys he hadde as smal as hath a goot.   690
No berd hadde he, ne never sholde have,
As smothe it was as it were late y-shave;
I trowe he were a gelding or a mare.
But of his craft, fro Berwik into Ware,
Ne was ther swich another pardoner.
For in his male he hadde a pilwe-beer,
Which that, he seyde, was our lady veyl:
He seyde, he hadde a gobet of the seyl
That sëynt Peter hadde, whan that he wente
Up-on the see, til Iesu Crist him hente.   700
He hadde a croys of latoun, ful of stones,
And in a glas he hadde pigges bones.

This Pardoner's hair was as yellow as wax but hung as smoothly as a skein of flax. It fell in bunches of thin locks which spread down over his shoulders. For greater comfort he didn't wear his hood but carried it bundled up in his bag. He thought he rode in the newest way. He rode with his hair hanging loose, save for his cap. His eyes started like a hare's. He had sewn a souvenir medal of St Veronica on his cap. His wallet lay in his lap in front of him and was brimful of pardons come piping hot from Rome. He had a feeble, goat-like voice. He had no beard, nor was ever likely to have. He was as smooth as if he had been freshly shaven. I think he was a gelding or a mare. Nonetheless, as far as his trade goes, there was no other pardoner like him from Berwick to Ware. In his bag he had a pillowcase which he claimed was the veil of the Blessed Virgin Mary. He said he had a piece of the sail that belonged to St Peter at the time he walked on the Sea of Galilee till Jesus Christ saved him. He had a pinchbeck cross full of stones and pigs' bones in a glass.

A vernicle: This he would have got from Rome. St Veronica (from which the word 'vernicle' comes) wiped Christ's face with her veil on the road to Calvary. The image was miraculously preserved and kept in St Peter's. The Pardoner's badge is a souvenir of this.

a gelding or a mare: Chaucer believes the Pardoner to be impotent.

pilwe-beer . . . pigges bones: The relics of saints are held to work miracles and, if prayed to devoutly, to secure the welfare of the soul. Of course, it was very easy to fake such relics. The purpose of the Canterbury pilgrimage was to visit the shrine of St Thomas à Becket whose relics are preserved there.

But with thise relikes, whan that he fond
A povre person dwelling up-on lond,
Up-on a day he gat him more moneye
Than that the person gat in monthes tweye.
And thus, with feyned flaterye and Iapes,
He made the person and the peple his apes.
But trewely to tellen, atte laste,
He was in chirche a noble ecclesiaste.   710
Wel coude he rede a lessoun or a storie,
But alderbest he song an offertorie;
For wel he wiste, whan that song was songe,
He moste preche, and wel affyle his tonge,
To winne silver, as he ful wel coude;
Therefore he song so meriely and loude.

   Now have I told you shortly, in a clause,
Thestat, tharray, the nombre, and eek the cause
Why that assembled was this companye
In Southwerk, at this gentil hostelrye,   720
That highte the Tabard, faste by the Belle.
But now is tyme to yow for to telle
How that we baren us that ilke night,
Whan we were in that hostelrye alight.
And after wol I telle of our viage,
And al the remenaunt of our pilgrimage.
But first I pray yow, of your curteisye,
That ye narette it nat my vileinye,
Thogh that I pleynly speke in this matere,
To telle yow hir wordes and hir chere;   730

With these relics, when he discovered a poor parson living in the countryside, he earned more money in one day than that parson earned in two months. Thus, with flattering lies and tricks, he made dupes of the parson and his flock. But, finally and honestly, he was an excellent religious officer in church. He could read a lesson or a saint's legend but best of all was his singing of the offertory, for he knew very well that once the anthem was over he must preach and smooth his tongue to earn money as best he could. Therefore he sang the more cheerfully and loudly.

Now I have told you, in a few words, the status, attire, number and also the reason why this company was gathered together at that excellent inn called the Tabard, near the Bell in Southwark. This is now the point at which to tell you how we passed our time that night when we had all arrived at the inn, then I'll describe our journey and the remainder of our pilgrimage. But first I beg you, of your courtesy, not to call it ill-breeding on my part when I speak bluntly about all this and tell you what they said and what they were like, nor if I repeat their words exactly.

person: 'parson' not 'person'.

offertorie: the part of the service at which the offering was made (see notes to l.452).

But first I pray yow . . .: Chaucer's audience was mainly aristocratic and belonged to the court (see p. 8). The great majority of his pilgrims do not. Since he wishes to be realistic he must use something near to the actual language of people like his characters. He hopes this will not be discourteous or even embarrassing to his courtly audience.

Ne thogh I speke hir wordes properly.
For this ye knowen al-so wel as I,
Who-so shal telle a tale after a man,
He moot reherce, as ny as ever he can,
Everich a word, if it be in his charge,
Al speke he never so rudeliche and large;
Or elles he moot telle his tale untrewe,
Or feyne thing, or finde wordes newe.
He may nat spare, al-thogh he were his brother;
He moot as wel seye o word as another.   740
Crist spak him-self ful brode in holy writ,
And wel ye woot, no vileinye is it.
Eek Plato seith, who-so that can him rede,
The wordes mote be cosin to the dede.
Also I prey yow to foryeve it me,
Al have I nat set folk in hir degree
Here in this tale, as that they sholde stonde;
My wit is short, ye may wel understonde.

  Greet chere made our hoste us everichon,
And to the soper sette he us anon;   750
And served us with vitaille at the beste.
Strong was the wyn, and wel to drinke us leste.

You know as well as I do that whoever wants to tell a story he has heard from someone else must retell every word of it as faithfully as he can, however coarsely and freely the first teller spoke. If he doesn't, a man must tell the story falsely, make things up or find new words. He can't hold back even if he is repeating his brother's words. He must include everything. Christ himself spoke openly and unaffectedly in the Bible, and you know very well there is no discourtesy there. Also, Plato says – to those who can read him – that words must be closely related to facts and deeds. I also ask you to forgive me for not having placed my characters here in the true social order in which they should be seen. You will appreciate that my insight is limited.

Our Host entertained us excellently and soon took us in to supper. He served us with the best food. The wine was strong and very much to our liking.

Crist spak ...: Christ did not use high-flown phrases when teaching. Chaucer will follow his example here.

Plato: a Greek philosopher. Knowledge of ancient Greek was very unusual in England in the Middle Ages. Chaucer could not read it and derived his quotation from a Latin source

wordes mote be ...: Language should reflect accurately what it describes: low language for low people, something more sophisticated for the more educated.

My wit is short ...: The modesty is ironic.

vitaille at the beste: Note how all through these lines, although Harry Bailey is sociable and even hearty, he is also careful to make sure he gets as much money as he can from the pilgrims. The prize dinner, for example, will be held in the Tabard.

A semely man our hoste was with-alle
For to han been a marshal in an halle;
A large man he was with eyen stepe,
A fairer burgeys is ther noon in Chepe:
Bold of his speche, and wys, and wel y-taught,
And of manhod him lakkede right naught.
Eek therto he was right a mery man,
And after soper pleyen he bigan,   760
And spak of mirthe amonges othere thinges,
Whan that we hadde maad our rekeninges;
And seyde thus: 'Now, lordinges, trewely,
Ye been to me right welcome hertely:
For by my trouthe, if that I shal nat lye,
I ne saugh this yeer so mery a companye
At ones in this herberwe as is now.
Fayn wolde I doon yow mirthe, wiste I how.
And of a mirthe I am right now bithoght,
To doon yow ese, and it shal coste noght.   770
    Ye goon to Caunterbury; God yow spede,
The blisful martir quyte yow your mede.
And wel I woot, as ye goon by the weye,
Ye shapen yow to talen and to pleye;
For trewely, confort ne mirthe is noon
To ryde by the weye doumb as a stoon;
And therfore wol I maken yow disport,
As I seyde erst, and doon yow som confort.
And if yow lyketh alle, by oon assent,
Now for to stonden at my Iugement,   780
And for to werken as I shal yow seye,
To-morwe, whan ye ryden by the weye,
Now, by my fader soule, that is deed,
But ye be merye, I wol yeve yow myn heed.
Hold up your hond, withouten more speche.'
    Our counseil was nat longe for to seche;

Our Host was a polite enough man to have acted as the major-domo in a Guildhall. He was a large fellow with bright eyes – there is not a finer citizen in the whole of Cheapside. Forthright, intelligent and experienced, he lacked none of the qualities of a very fine man. In addition, he was a sociable fellow, and, after supper, he began to relax and spoke of happiness among other things (when we had all paid our bills) and he said: 'Now, gentlemen, upon my word, you are heartily welcome here. Truthfully, upon my honour, I haven't seen so jolly a company altogether in this place all year as there is now. I would gladly make you happy if I knew how. And I have just thought of something that will. It will bring you pleasure and cost you nothing.

'You are going to Canterbury – God speed you, and the holy martyr duly reward you! I know very well that as you make your journey you plan to gossip and relax, for, to be honest, there is no pleasure in riding along as dumb as a stone. So, I'll provide you with some entertainment, as I've just said, and give you some pleasure. If you all agree to bide by my decision and to do as I say, tomorrow, while you ride along, now, by my dead father's soul, strike me dead, if you're not made cheerful! Let's have a show of hands and no more talk.'

We didn't have to think the matter over for very long.

herberwe: harbour. The word has occurred before in the description of the Shipman. Here it is used metaphorically.

yeve yow myn heed: give you my head, i.e. I am confident I will make you merry.

Us thoughte it was noght worth to make it wys,
And graunted him withouten more avys,
And bad him seye his verdit, as him leste.
   'Lordinges,' quod he, 'now herkneth for the beste;   790
But tak it not, I prey yow, in desdeyn;
This is the poynt, to speken short and pleyn,
That ech of yow, to shorte with your weye,
In this viage, shal telle tales tweye,
To Caunterbury-ward, I mene it so,
And hom-ward he shal tellen othere two,
Of aventures that whylom han bifalle.
And which of yow that bereth him best of alle,
That is to seyn, that telleth in this cas
Tales of best sentence and most solas,   800
Shal have a soper at our aller cost
Here in this place, sitting by this post,
Whan that we come agayn fro Caunterbury.
And for to make yow the more mery,
I wol my-selven gladly with yow ryde,
Right at myn owne cost, and be your gyde.
And who-so wol my Iugement withseye
Shal paye al that we spenden by the weye.
And if ye vouche-sauf that it be so,
Tel me anon, with-outen wordes mo,   810
And I wol erly shape me therfore.'

We didn't believe it was worth mulling over, and so we let him go on without another thought and asked him to tell us what he had in mind.

'Gentlemen,' he said, 'listen carefully, but I beg you not to despise what I have to say. To be brief about it, this is the nub of the matter: each of you, to shorten the journey, shall tell two tales on the way to Canterbury – that's what I suggest – and on the way home tell two more about events that have happened at some time or another. And the one who acquits himself best – that is to say, who tells under these circumstances the most instructive and amusing tale, shall be bought supper at our common expense, here, in this inn, when we have returned from Canterbury. And, to make you all the more happy, I myself will readily go with you at my own expense and be your guide. Whoever contradicts my decisions shall pay for everything that we spend along the way and, if you agree that things shall be done like this, tell me now without further discussion and I'll go off at once and get ready.'

to shorte with your weye: Each pilgrim would tell two stories on the way out and two on the return. Chaucer says there were twenty-nine pilgrims. In fact with attendants, himself and Harry Bailey there were thirty-two and they were joined by the Canon and the Canon's Yeoman later. This would have made an anthology of approximately one hundred and thirty-six stories. In fact, there are twenty-four in various states of completion.

best sentence and most solas: The tales should instruct and entertain.

our aller cost: The pilgrims would club together to buy the winner's supper.

This thing was graunted, and our othes swore
With ful glad herte, and preyden him also
That he wold vouche-sauf for to do so,
And that he wolde been our governour,
And of our tales Iuge and reportour,
And sette a soper at a certeyn prys;
And we wold reuled been at his devys,
In heigh and lowe; and thus, by oon assent,
We been acorded to his Iugement.   820
And ther-up-on the wyn was fet anon;
We dronken, and to reste wente echon,
With-outen any lenger taryinge.
   A-morwe, whan that day bigan to springe,
Up roos our host, and was our aller cok,
And gadrede us togidre, alle in a flok,
And forth we riden, a litel more than pas,
Un-to the watering of seint Thomas.
And there our host bigan his hors areste,
And seyde; 'Lordinges, herkneth, if yow leste.   830
Ye woot your forward, and I it yow recorde.
If even-song and morwe-song acorde,
Lat se now who shal telle the firste tale.
As ever mote I drinke wyn or ale,
Who-so be rebel to my Iugement
Shal paye for al that by the weye is spent.
Now draweth cut, er that we ferrer twinne;
He which that hath the shortest shal biginne.

The proposal was adopted. We gladly swore to it and asked him to act as he had said he would and be our leader, adjudicator and umpire, and arrange a supper at a fixed price, while we would all follow his directions. Thus we unanimously agreed to his plan. After that the wine was brought. We drank and then each of us went to bed without delay.

The following morning, at daybreak, our Host rose, woke us all and gathered us together in a flock and we rode forth at little more than walking pace to St Thomas's watering hole. There our Host reined in his horse and said: 'Gentlemen, listen please. You know your agreement. I now remind you of it. If what was said last night agrees with what is thought this morning, let's now see who's going to tell the first story. As I hope always to drink wine or ale, whoever rebels against my decisions shall pay for everything we spend along the route. Now, we'll draw lots before we go any further. He who draws the shortest straw shall start.

our aller cok: The cockerel crowing marks the start of day. Harry Bailey wakes them all.

the watering of seint Thomas: a place to water horses. These were common on well-used routes.

even-song and morwe-song: vespers and matins, but here used metaphorically to suggest what was said the evening before and whether it still holds now, the following day.

As ever mote I drinke: a fitting oath for a publican.

Sire knight,' quod he, 'my maister and my lord,
Now draweth cut, for that is myn acord.   840
Cometh neer,' quod he, 'my lady prioresse;
And ye, sir clerk, lat be your shamfastnesse,
Ne studieth noght; ley hond to, every man.'

   Anon to drawen every wight bigan,
And shortly for to tellen, as it was,
Were it by aventure, or sort, or cas,
The sothe is this, the cut fil to the knight,
Of which ful blythe and glad was every wight;
And telle he moste his tale, as was resoun,
By forward and by composicioun,   850
As ye han herd; what nedeth wordes mo?
And whan this gode man saugh it was so,
As he that wys was and obedient
To kepe his forward by his free assent,
He seyde: 'Sin I shal biginne the game,
What, welcome be the cut, a Goddes name!
Now lat us ryde, and herkneth what I seye.'

   And with that word we riden forth our weye;
And he bigan with right a mery chere
His tale anon, and seyde in this manere.   860

Sir Knight,' he said, 'my master and my lord, draw your lot, for that's what I say. Come near,' said he, 'Madame Prioress. And you, Sir Clerk, don't be shy and stop your thinking. Let's about it, all of you!'

There and then everybody started to draw his lot and, to tell briefly what happened, whether it was chance or fate or it just happened that way, the fact is that the Knight drew the shortest straw, which pleased everybody. He had to tell his tale as had been agreed and as you have heard. What more needs to be said? When this good man saw how things had fallen out, since he was wise and considerate enough to keep freely to the agreement, he said: 'Since I'm to begin the game, why, by the Lord, this cut is very welcome! Now, let's ride on and listen to what I have to say.' With that, we rode forth and he began at once to tell his tale in a cheerful manner, as you shall hear.

knight ... prioresse ... clerk: Representation of the actively secular, churchly and the scholarly worlds respectively.

aventure, or sort, or cas: similar ideas of chance. There is no implication that the drawing of straws was rigged. We start, nonetheless, with the pilgrim of the highest social status.

Themes

CHARACTERIZATION

The means of characterization in the *General Prologue* are many and subtle. The hierarchies of feudalism and the Church provide one system – we know who is socially superior to whom and so on – though this is not something Chaucer employs in a simple way. At the close of the *General Prologue* he asks his audience to forgive him for not describing people in the correct order of social precedence. Of course, this is ironic. Chaucer knew very well that there are other equally interesting ways of looking at people besides their place in society. Different people have different degrees of liveliness and are more and less interesting than others, for example. These qualities do not necessarily correspond to their station in life. Who is to say which is the more interesting character, the Knight or the Miller, the Wife of Bath or the Prioress, the Shipman or the Franklin? In this section it may be useful to look at three ways in which Chaucer characterizes the pilgrims: their clothes, their physical appearance and their professions.

Dress

One of the first and most immediate ways in which we tend to judge a person is by the way in which he or she dresses. We are fortunate in living in a time when this is quite as varied as it has ever been. A walk down the main street of any town will reveal a rich variety of styles of dress and haircut among the different sexes, age-groups and classes. The same is true when we look at the Canterbury pilgrims.

The Wife of Bath is the most gawdy example of someone whose personality is partly defined through her clothes. Her scarlet stockings, huge hat and cascade of wimples suggest her wonderfully extrovert and sensuous character. They also suggest her class. Here is a woman who is obviously rich, passionate and worldly. The Prioress, on the other hand, is dressed in the habit which, strictly speaking, belonged to her Order. But notice how it reflects her ladylike nature. It is neat and clean, while the pleats in her wimple suggest her refinement of manner. Here, in her clothes, we see a woman who is, at the same time, a member of the Church and a woman of breeding.

The Squire and the Pardoner form another interesting pair. The Squire's richly embroidered coat reveals both his social standing and his young and amorous nature. Slightly comic though its over-elaboration is, the embroideries suggest the potency of spring, which Chaucer evokes in the opening of his poem. The Pardoner, on the other hand, is a pathetic creature: possibly impotent but a would-be lover. His efforts to look the height of fashion result in his seeming merely absurd.

Chaucer greatly admired men of professional skill and he often uses their clothes to suggest this. The humility and practical nature of the Knight are suggested by his dirty surcoat. The competence of the Knight's Yeoman and his contentment with his place in life are clear in his bright, trim clothes and accessories. The Physician's clothes suggest the discreet luxury of a successful professional man.

The rather anonymous quality of the five Guildsmen is brought out by their all being dressed in the livery of one company. Two middle-class characters whom Chaucer particularly admired are also in part characterized by their clothing: the silk band with its thin coloured stripes gives the Sergeant of the Law a special touch of individuality, while the white silk purse of the Franklin suggests something of his opulent delight in life, the self-indulgence of a wealthy but, as we also learn, socially aware man.

Clothes also add to the sense of colour in the *General Prologue*. In addition to the garish colours of the clothes worn by the Wife of Bath, we might recall the white coat and blue hood of the Miller and such items of jewellery as the Yeoman's medal of St Christopher, the Prioress's rosary and the Monk's brooch, all of which again provide both concrete detail and a comment on those wearing them.

Physical Details

Some of the characters in the *General Prologue* are defined almost entirely by their tasks or social position. For example, we do not know what the Sergeant of the Law, the Guildsmen or the Manciple look like. Others are vivid physical presences. We recall the weather-beaten skin of the Yeoman and the Shipman, the emaciated Clerk, the shining face of the Monk and the twinkling eyes of the Friar. The thinness of the Reeve suggests much about his character, while it is a pleasant touch that the refined Prioress is, nonetheless, a rather large lady.

It is often Chaucer's rogues who are most vividly characterized through their bodies. Both the Monk and the Friar, as we have seen, are active physical presences. The Wife of Bath (no rogue, perhaps, but certainly no better than she needs to be) has gaps between her teeth, broad hips and a rubicund face. The Cook has a growth on his shin, something that strikes us as particularly repulsive in the light of his job. But the three characters whose physical details most readily stick in the mind are the Miller, the Summoner and the Pardoner. Indeed, the physical details Chaucer provides give an element of caricature to each of these characters. The muscle-bound Miller with his fox-red beard and the wart on his nose with its bristling hairs, the Summoner with his disgusting skin and fiery cherubim's face pierced with lecherous eyes, the Pardoner with his repulsive hair and staring glance, all these are larger than life. Their very physical grossness suggests what low characters they are, and the degree of caricature reflects their natures and makes us smile at the aptness of the physical presence which Chaucer gives them.

As with all Chaucer's vivid physical detail, the aspects of people's appearance that he chooses to emphasize tell us a great deal about what they are like and how he would wish us to evaluate them.

The Pilgrims' Professions

Most of us are defined to a greater or lesser extent by the job we do. In some cases this has a marked effect on the way we behave. We expect a doctor to be kindly and efficient, a lawyer to be judicious, a priest to be reserved and pious. Indeed, so strong are the pre-conceptions we have about the ways in which some people should behave that we are mildly shocked when they do not conform to what we expect. This is something Chaucer relies on in presenting his gallery of portraits. The little worldly vanities of the Prioress, for example, do not measure up to the ideal view of how such women should behave. Though it was a convention to attack the worldliness of monks and friars, Chaucer's characters are so vividly alive that their failure to live up to expectations is particularly powerful.

Other people are so close to what we expect that there is a particularly comforting feeling about them. Chaucer's idealized characters, of course, are all of this type. The Knight, the Yeoman, the Clerk, the Parson and the Ploughman are all defined by what they do, and what they do is excellently performed. There is a feeling of correctness and calm dignity about these men. They are all members of worthy if socially diverse trades and professions, but the honesty of each, the feeling that they contribute to the common good, is heartening in each case.

A few of the characters are so defined by the requirements of their work that, rather than appearing simply as confident, well-balanced people, they seem almost to have disappeared into their professions. This is particularly true of the money-conscious middle classes. The Merchant, for example, brings everything he talks about round to amassing wealth, while the five Guildsmen form an introverted, enclosed little group that Chaucer looks on with rather wry contempt. Not all professions fulfil an individual's need to become a complete person.

Professional rogues form a group by themselves. We have mentioned the Monk and the Friar, but we should notice how the Summoner and the Pardoner seem largely to derive their disreputable characters from their disreputable jobs.

There is, thus, a wide variety of ways in which Chaucer discusses his pilgrims' professions. Those which are honest and skilful and contribute to knowledge or the public good he admires, though he also has a sneaking admiration for those who are skilful but dishonest. The former give an enhanced sense of dignity, while the latter provide a feeling of raucous, human life.

MONEY

A great many of the pilgrims are characterized through their attitude to money. We can perhaps most usefully define this under three headings: those who are idealistic, those who serve or belong to the wealthy and professional classes, and those whose interest in money ranges through the mild snobbery of affluence to being downright grasping rogues. Clearly in a poem as subtle and complex as this, such divisions are not watertight.

The idealists are partly united by the fact that money and the social prestige it may bring are not their chief concerns. They do not seem to be a major interest of the Knight's, for example, though he is the senior pilgrim socially and, doubtless, a man of considerable means. Like the others of this group, he is interested in higher things. The Clerk personifies this particularly clearly. Study is his whole life. He needs money to pursue this but spends it on books rather than himself. Both he and his horse are undernourished. All that he can obtain from his friends is spent on books and, in return, the Clerk prays for the good of his benefactors' souls. Chaucer ironically compares him to the alchemists, who made themselves poor in their search for wealth. The interests of the Clerk, however, are wholly other-worldly, and in this he is like the Parson. To the Parson, money and the position and comfort it may bring mean nothing. He is poor, generous and exclusively concerned with the welfare of his parishioners' souls. He would more readily give them money than excommunicate them for failing to pay their tithes. He is not tempted by the soft and easy life that more lucrative positions in the Church could bring him. Ironically, he himself is compared to gold: the metal that does not corrupt. The Parson, however, has no wish to convert such gold into coins. Gold is a metaphor for his sincerity, not a description of his desires. Similarly with the Ploughman. He again is poor, but, rather than striving to increase his wealth, he helps those less fortunate than himself and pays his taxes regularly to the Church. Those whom Chaucer paints as idealistic neither wholly despise money nor seek to hoard it. They all live by higher ideals than the pursuit of wealth provides and are uncorrupted by the love of money because they are indifferent to what it can buy. For all of these men true charity is far more important.

Not everyone is called to such idealism and two such rich men whom Chaucer describes wholly favourably are the Sergeant of the Law and the Franklin. The first is an impressively intelligent professional man whose skills have made him wealthy. While he is not obsessed by money he is, nonetheless, busily buying himself into the landed gentry. To this class, too, belongs the Franklin, a man of ample means who, while he spends his wealth on enhancing his life, is, nonetheless, far from money-grabbing. Rather, he uses the position and affluence he has for public service and the common good. Lastly, we should perhaps add to this group the curious figure of the Manciple who, while certainly not a grand man, is an honest professional, one who is quite as skilled as those he serves. His pride lies not in making money for himself, but, rather, in his exceptional talent at looking after the funds entrusted to him. He is highly efficient but, unlike the Reeve, not corrupted by the power such control may bring him.

The love of money is the root of all evil: such, ironically, is the moral of the *Pardoner's Tale*. The love of money and the position it brings do indeed corrupt, and Chaucer shows this in varying degrees, from the Prioress who, with her ladylike manners and mild worldly vanities is hardly an evil creature, down through the corrupt clergy, the purse-conscious middle classes, to such grasping rascals as the Pardoner himself.

Chaucer shows that many of the pilgrims attached to the Church have been corrupted by worldliness. There is, as we have seen, mild criticism in the portrait of the Prioress, far more in the portrait of the Friar, whose love of money has hardened his heart against the call of such really needy people as beggarwomen and lepers. However, while the criticism of these two men is somewhat offset by Chaucer's relish of their sheer vitality, the Merchant and the five Guildsmen are shown to have been made rather faceless by their obsessive concern with wealth. This is particularly clear in the portrait of the Merchant. Money is the sole topic of his conversation and goal of his energies, while the Guildsmen and, even more, their snobby wives, are obsessed with the money they have and their hopes of the social position this will bring them. Indeed, they are presented as characterless, rather absurd and, in the end, vulgar. To be sure, they are wealthy, but their money does not expand their personalities and it is not used in a way that serves the public good. In the end they emerge as rather anonymous people. Nonetheless, Chaucer is neither simple nor dismissive in his view of the money-conscious middle classes. The Wife of Bath, for example, is certainly rich and she makes sure she gets the recognition she thinks her wealth deserves. But, while she is very conscious of this – vain, ostentatious and proud – she is far more interesting than the Guildsmen's wives, for example. The prestige that money brings her and on which she insists is merely part of her far wider lively, worldly, sensuous character. The Wife of Bath is not ultimately defined by her attitude to money; it is merely an element in her portrait.

The Physician, while a learned man and far from being wholly a rogue, has a great love of money. His considerable skills make him, no doubt, worthy of what he earns, but there is no doubt either that he is grasping and somewhat corrupt. The Miller, too, is greedy and dishonest. He is quite happy to steal, as is the Shipman. But both men are excused for this: the Miller by his natural vigour, the Shipman by his skills. The love of money corrupts, but it does not have to corrupt absolutely.

In contrast to these two men, we should look at the Reeve: a bitter and suspicious man. There is no sense of joy or robust life about his concern with money. Neither is there the warming sense of true managerial skills efficiently employed, as there is with the Manciple. The Reeve is a scheming, dishonest man, a selfish and domineering person whose love of money has nothing life-enhancing about it at all. People are afraid of him. His ruthless efficiency screens his own double-dealing. His money is secretly hoarded (many of the other crooks, one feels, at least spend what they get and try to enjoy their wealth) and there is about him the chilling feeling that money means power and is something to relish for its own sake.

However, it is in the lower orders of the Church that the love of money causes the worst abuses. We have already seen how the love of money has damaged such figures as the Monk and, even more so, the Friar, both of whom were supposedly committed to a life of poverty. Their wealth has encouraged them to break the other vows of their vocation: chastity and obedience. With the Summoner and the Pardoner we see money and religion in a wholly corrupt alliance. Both men believe that the most important aspect of the Christian life – the forgiveness of sins through the sacraments of the Church – is no more than a matter of cash. The Summoner accepts bribes and says quite openly that forgiveness can always be bought at a price. Excommunication, he says, is nothing to be frightened of. A man can pay his way out of it. Chaucer strongly disagrees with him.

The most completely mercenary member of this group is the Pardoner. To modern eyes he appears particularly shocking. He not only sells certificates of forgiveness, thereby reducing the forgiveness of sins to a purely financial transaction, but trades off the credulity of innocent and gullible people by peddling relics in a thoroughly calculating and dishonest way. At first sight, the Pardoner is the most blatantly and odiously hypocritical member of the entire pilgrimage and, in many respects, it is hard to forgive him. Nonetheless, in characteristic fashion, Chaucer does not wholly condemn him. To ply his trade effectively the Pardoner must encourage people's faith, and this he does. The congregation's devotion is increased by his sermons so that, ironically, the Pardoner does, in the end, work for the good of the Christian faith.

The last full portrait Chaucer offers in the *General Prologue* is of the Host, Harry Bailey. He is an attractive, extrovert figure, rather domineering perhaps, but essentially a fine man. Like all the characters Chaucer admires, Harry Bailey shares his vigorous nature with everyone. Of all the pilgrims, he is the one who most enhances our sense of energetic life. But it is important to recognize that he, too, is by no means indifferent to money. He begins to entertain the company only when they have paid their bills and, while he suggests the idea of story-telling, he is careful to ensure that the prize is a dinner paid for by the whole company and held at his own tavern. The pilgrimage is certainly financially advantageous for him. Chaucer makes quite sure we realize this. But, finally, money is not his only or exclusive concern. He is motivated at least as much by his naturally warm and sociable nature as he is by money. It is such vitality that Chaucer admires.

Thus, while it is shown that the love of money often corrupts, Chaucer's view of money and the power it brings is as subtle and humane as his view of life itself.

THE CHURCH

Chaucer was a devout Christian which meant, of course, that he was a devout Catholic. It is important to realize this if we are to understand his attitude to the Church properly. Chaucer knew that the Church was riddled with abuses but he was also sure that its teaching contained the fundamental truths of human life.

We should begin our discussion of the Church with the Parson. He is held up as an example of how a man of the Church should live. The Parson's entire life is a pursuit of the goals of his vocation – the spiritual welfare of the souls in his parish. To be effective he must set a good example and his clean life of active charity does just this. Far from being tempted by the lure of London and a comfortable and easy living, Chaucer shows the Parson as energetic, active in all seasons, concerned, humane and sincere. Nothing keeps him from fulfilling his duty. His parish is large and widely spread out. Nonetheless, he visits everyone, rich and poor, regardless of the state of the weather or his own health. His charity, unlike the Prioress's, is not sentimental. The Parson is a forthright man who speaks his mind to sinners. The overall impression we have of him is of someone who is tough and sincere, a believer untroubled by religious doubts and, above all, a man to whom faith is a way of life. It is this solidness, the direct translation of thought into works, that so impresses Chaucer. The truly spiritual man is not grand, pretentious or extreme. He is an honest worker and an example of straightforward faith and charity.

Such values are not adhered to by any of the other Churchmen. They are, by and large, worldly and money-conscious and concerned with display, pleasure and success. The Monk, for example, whose impressive physical presence we might admire in another context, has flouted his vows of poverty, obedience and chastity. He is wealthy, he ignores the rules, and the love-knot on his brooch casts some doubt on his chastity. The Friar is worse. He is a feckless and gossiping womanizer, a drinker, a skilled exploiter of even the poorest, a man hardened against charity. He abuses the wide powers of confession he has gained by, quite simply, selling forgiveness. He is not interested in the state of the sinner's soul but only in the weight of his purse. Such abuse is even more pronounced, of course, in the characters of the Summoner and the Pardoner. The Summoner's abuses draw from Chaucer a strong statement of personal belief. He may allow himself to agree with the Monk on the limits of the usefulness of monasteries but, when the Summoner declares that excommunication is nothing to be particularly concerned about, then Chaucer steps in and contradicts. In his view, to be cut off from forgiveness and the sacraments of the Church is a very serious matter indeed. The right of the Church to inflict such a punishment is unquestioned. It is not – or should not be – a matter of the sinner merely paying his way out. The fate of the soul is in question.

Criticisms such as this, however, are only part of Chaucer's presentation of the Church. He comments, but he rarely judges. This is more than mere benevolence and a relish for the spice of life – though Chaucer certainly had both – it is a matter of faith. It is for God, not man, to condemn. A man's duty is to forgive sinners and enemies and to try and live in harmony with his fellows. Chaucer's humanity lies (in part at least) in his humour and in his unaffected kindliness, which stem both from his Christian faith and his richly matured experience of life.

Thus Chaucer was fully aware of the abuses in the Church while, at the same time, he believed in the Church's fundamental sanctity. He presents a variety of corrupt Church people – their corruption ranging from mild vanity to outright heresy – but he presents only one ideal Churchman. We should note, however, that he *does* present three worthy Christians who did not hold office in the Church: the Knight, the Clerk and the Ploughman.

These three come from different areas of society – the nobility, the world of learning and the labouring class. Each has dignity. The Knight, for example, impresses us with his natural bearing which is underscored by a genuine humility. Here is a figure in whom the chivalric and Christian ideals are in harmony. The Knight's active life has largely been spent in fighting religious wars and, as with the other worthy laymen, much of his dignity derives from his apparent idealism.

The Clerk, too, can be seen as a great idealist. Study is his life and it should be noted that such study enhances his faith and deepens his moral outlook. He prays for those who give him the wherewithal to study and what he does have – his knowledge – he shares in the proper Christian way.

It is the Ploughman who is perhaps the most familiar example of the perfect Christian: hardworking and at peace with the world. Patient and long-suffering, he loves God wholeheartedly and at all times, while his charity to his neighbours shows that he loves them as he loves himself. In addition, he is loyal to the Church, paying his tithes fully and on time. There is about him that sense of honest contentment that marks out the true Christian.

Finally, we should notice that, for all their diversity, each of Chaucer's characters is on a pilgrimage. The point is an obvious one, but it is sometimes forgotten that the purpose of a pilgrimage is to quicken faith and thank God and the saints for favours received. The idea of drawing all these people together in this way does suggest the ideal which most invisibly but surely unites them: the fact that, regardless of weaknesses and social status, they are all Christian men and women gathered together for a pious purpose. Taken all together, Chaucer's cavalcade of pilgrims is a picture of the whole of English medieval society united for the glorification of God and his saints.

THE LAYMEN

We have seen that three of Chaucer's laymen (people who were not members of the priesthood or monastic orders) were virtuous Christians, while only one of the Churchmen wholly lived up to the ideals of the faith. All the pilgrims, nonetheless, are drawn into a communal assertion of faith and praise which is what the pilgrimage is all about.

A great many of Chaucer's characters belong to the secular world and, in their various ways, reveal the wealth and colour of medieval society. The Squire is one such character.

The Squire is a handsome young lover on the verge of manhood. He is a representative of the fashionable courtly life – a way of life with which Chaucer was wholly familiar. As we see from the Squire, this life centred around the cultivation of the arts and military skills and was fuelled by the desire to seem worthy of a lady's love. It is a highly colourful, highly refined world of youth and beauty in which the Squire is obviously at home.

Chaucer has varying degrees of respect for his middle-class pilgrims. He values intelligence, skill and concern for the common good. The Franklin, for example, personifies the type of men who were slowly evolving into the English squirearchy: men of wealth and talent, landowners with a vested interest in the stability of the country. Chaucer's Franklin – while thoroughly appreciating the good things of life in a way that the poet himself finds delightful – is clearly a man who expects order and efficient administration. These certainly exist in his own house, but his energy and concern lead him to use his talents in public life. He is a Justice of the Peace, a Member of Parliament and has held a number of senior positions in county administration. The Franklin is extrovert, confident and relishes life.

Chaucer was, as we have seen, impressed by professionalism, whether that of the Knight (which was wholly worthy) or that of the Churchmen (which often was not). The Sergeant of the Law is a man of learning and this, coupled with his skills and experience, invites some degree of respect. Nevertheless, this does not blind Chaucer to his small pretensions: his desire to appear hard-worked when this was clearly not the case. Here we see a man who, rather as Chaucer himself had done, has risen nearly to the top of his profession through intelligence and sheer hard work. The man is to be trusted and respected. Chaucer tells us that he is busily buying his way into the landed gentry, and this was true of the Sergeant's whole class. Notice that the Sergeant is a wealthy man and one who has made his money largely by his own efforts. Money, nonetheless, is not something that wholly obsesses him.

Such respect is not extended to the Merchant and the Guildsmen. They are representatives of the City rich, and Chaucer's slightly patronizing tone may reflect an antagonism between the Court and the new merchant classes. All these men are rather faceless and obsessed by money and status. In particular, the ghastly snobbery of the Guildsmen's wives is a picture reminiscent of the aspiration of the newly rich in any period.

The laymen of lowest social standing in the *General Prologue* are the Cook, the Shipman, the Ploughman, the Miller, the Manciple and the Reeve. They form a various group.

Both the Manciple and the Reeve are administrators; today they might be described as 'middle management'. The first is a fine man in his way: efficient and shrewd when it comes to catering for his masters. He is wholly defined by his skills. The men he serves are qualified to do similar administration but on a far larger scale. They could run the estates of the greater nobility or attend to the business of a whole shire. Chaucer's delicate insight has perceived, however, that, in his way, the unlettered Manciple is more proficient than all of them. The Reeve contrasts very unfavourably with the Manciple. Although he, too, is successful (as shown by his material gains), how unattractive is this thin, suspicious and chilling figure, who is mildly dishonest himself while keeping an eagle eye on the dishonesties of others. Those below him are scared to death of him. The Reeve is a serf (this is indicated by his cropped hair) but he has, nonetheless, done well for himself. Chaucer tells us that he has a supply of cash hidden away, possibly in the pleasant, tree-shaded house that goes with his job. We are also told that the Reeve lends his master the man's own money without his being aware of it and always earns his thanks for doing so. The Reeve is rather isolated socially and his position at the end of the procession of pilgrims mirrors this.

The Miller is a wonderful character: enormously strong, foul-mouthed and dishonest. Much of the sense of caricature about him comes from Chaucer's emphasis on his physical characteristics. And we cannot help but share Chaucer's enjoyment of such a pleasant rogue who is, after all, as honest as a miller could traditionally be expected to be.

Finally, we must discuss Harry Bailey. Chaucer has presented us with a whole range of characters and, as the gallery of portraits is built up, so our sense of the wealth and diversity of medieval life is enhanced. Harry Bailey, the commandingly extrovert London publican, is a most appropriate figure to close with. And he is the one figure we see in action in the *General Prologue*. His genial forceful-ness is at once obvious to us. Here is a man who can lead others not by virtue of his social status but through sheer force of personality. It is this that makes him so admirable. To be sure, he is somewhat domineering and has an eye open to opportunities for making money, but, like all the characters Chaucer relishes, Harry Bailey has a vigorously social nature, an ebullient love of life with which he manages to draw a diverse group of pilgrims into a common purpose. And between the Tales his humour, his tact and his forcefulness will be needed frequently.

Glossary

a: in

a-morwe: on the following morning

a-sonder: apart

absolucion: absolution

accorde: agree

achat: purchase

achatours: purchasers

acordaunt: agreeable to

acorded: suitable

adrad: afraid

adversitee: adversity

aferd: afraid

affyle: make smooth

after oon: one invariable standard

after: according to

ageyn: against

alderbest: best of all

alderman: municipal or guild officer

ale-stake: a garland in front of an ale house

algate: always

Algezir: Algeciras

Alisaundre: Alexandria

aller: everybody's

alwey: always

alyght: alighted, staying

amblere: ambling horse easy to ride

amiable: friendly

anlas: a short two-edged knife or dagger

anon: soon

apes: dupes

apiked: trimmed

apothecaries: apothecaries or pharmacists (see textual note)

aqueyntaunce: associate with

areste: bring to a halt

aright: certainly

array: dress, clothing

arreage: arrears

Artoys: Artois

arwes: arrows

as nouthe: as of now, just now

ascendent: astrological term (see textual note)

assent: agreement, accord

assente: agree

assoilling: absolution

assyse: assizes

astored: provided

astronomye: astronomy

atones: at once, at one time

auditour: accountant

aught: all

Austin: Augustine

avaunce: profit

avaunt: boast

aventure: accident

avys: discussion

ay: always

baar: carried

bacheler: aspirant after knighthood

baggepype: bagpipes

baillif: superintendent, bailiff

bake: baked

balled: bald

bar: carried

baren: conducted

barres: small bands

batailles: combats

bathed: bathed

bawdrik: a belt worn across the chest and under the arm

bedes: beads, a rosary

beggestere: beggar woman

Belmarye: a heathen kingdom in Africa

ben: be

benefice: job as parish priest or other religious office

Beneit: Benedict

benigne: kindly

berd: beard

berye: berry

bever: beaver fur

bifel: befell, happened

biforn: before, in credit

binne: bin for storing grain

bisette: employed

bisier: busier

bisinesse: work

bismotered: dirtied

bisyde: near, the suburbs of

bit: bade

blankmanger: white meat with rice, milk, sugar and almonds

bledde: bleeding

blew: blue

blisful: blessedly happy

blithe: happy

bokeler, bokelor: small shield

Boloigne: Bologna

bootes: boots

boras: borax

bord: dais, table of state

y-bore: carried

born: conducted

bote: remedy

botes: boots

bracer: protector of the arm against bowstrings

braun: muscles

breed: bread

breem: bream (a fish)

breke: break

bret-ful: brimful

bretherhed: brotherhood, fraternity

brimstoon: sulphur

Britayne: Brittany

brode: broadly, in an uneducated way

broille: broil

brooch: brooch

brood: broad

brustles: bristles

brydel: bridal

brynge: call

Burdeux-ward: from Bordeaux

burdoun: refrain

burgeys: prosperous citizen

but it: unless
by cause: since
byte: cauterize
byynge: buying

caas: case
calf: calf, lower part of leg
can: knows about
cappe: out-caps them all or beats them
carf: carved
carie: lift
carl: fellow
carpe: chat animatedly
Cartage: Carthage, or Cartagena in Spain
cas: chance, instance
catel: possessions, property
caughte: took
ceint: girdle
celle: small monastery
certeyn: agreed, fixed, certainly
ceruce: salve made of white lead
chambres: rooms
chaped: capped
chapman: merchant
y-chapped: capped
charitee: charity
chaunterie: endowed chapel where founder's soul is prayed for
chekes: cheeks
Chepe: Cheapside
chere: behaviour, entertainment
cherubines: like a cherubim or angel
chevisaunce: borrowing money on credit

chiknes: chickens
chirche: church
chivachye: deeds of arms
Christofre: a medallion of St Christopher
chyn: chin
chyvachie: cavalry expedition
clause: few words
clennesse: cleanliness
clense: cleanse
cleped: called, named
clerk: postgraduate scholar (see textual note)
cloysterer: monk in monastery
cofre: coffer
cok: cockerel
colerik: quick-tempered
Coloigne: Cologne
colpons: portions
y-come: come (past participle)
compaignye: company, close friends, lovers
complexioun: humour, temperament (see textual note)
composicioun: agreement
concubyn: mistress
condicioun: nature, inner and outer
conseil: secret intentions
contree: country, part of country, district
coold: cold
cop: top
cope: priest's cloak
coppe: cup, beaker
corage: heart
cordial: something that stimulates the heart

cosin: resemble, be at one with

cote: coat, outer garment

coude: know how to

countour: auditor of accounts

countrefete: imitate

cours: course or journey

couthe, as he: as best he could

couthe: known of

covenaunt: agreement

coverchiefs: kerchief, headscarves

covyne: deceitful agreement

coy: shy

Cristen: Christian

Cristendom: Christian countries

croppes: tips, shoots

crowned: with a crown on top

croys: cross

crulle: curled

cryke: creek

curat: parish priest

cure: care

curious: elaborate, knowledgeable

curs: curse

cursen: excommunicate

cursing: cursing

curteisye: courtesy

curteys: courteous

cut: lots drawn like straws

daliaunce: gossip

daunger: within his jurisdiction

daungerous: difficult to approach

dayerye: dairy

dayesye: daisy

deed: dead

deef: deaf

deeth: death (not necessarily the plague)

degree: social status

del: time

deliver: nimble, agile

delve: dig

delyt: pleasure

depe: deeply

Dertemouthe: Dartmouth

desdeyn: badly

despitous: full of contempt

dettelees: in credit

devys: direction

devyse: tell of

deyntee: thoroughbred

deyntees: dainties

deys: dais, raised platform

diete: diet

digestible: easily digested

digne (l. 519): scornful

digne (l. 141): worthy

diligent: attentive

diocyse: diocese (see textual note)

dischevele: with hair hanging loose

discreet: tactful

dispence: expenditure

disport: geniality, recreation, diversion

divyne: divine

dokked: tonsured, cropped

domes: judgements

dong: dung

doon: do

dooth: does

dore: door

dormant: permanent

dorste: dared, dare

doseyn: dozen

doumb: dumb

draughte: measure of drink

y-drawe: stolen
dresse: arrange, prepare, look after
drogges: drugs
droghte: drought, dryness
drye: dry
dwellynge: living
Dyere: a dyer of cloth
dyke: make ditches

ecclesiaste: churchman
eek: also
elles: else
ellis: else
embrouded: embroidered
encombred: stuck
endyte: compose, draw up, write
engendred: engendered, produced, begotten
enoynt: anointed
ensample: example
entuned: intoned
envyned: stored with wine
Epicurus: Epicurus: philosopher of pleasure
erchedekenes: archdeacon's (see textual note)
erst: before, just now
erys: ears
eschaunge: money-markets
esed: accommodated, entertained
estat: fettle, condition, social status
estatlich: stately
estatly: stately
esy: easy, undemanding, moderate
even-song: even-song, i.e. what was said last night

evene: ordinary, moderate
everich: each, every
everichon: everyone
evermore: always
everydeel: all of them
exemple: example
eyen: eyes

facultee: ability
fader: father
fair language: flattery
faire: elegantly, well
fairnesse: leading a good life
falding: coarse cloth
y-falle: fallen
famulier: well known to
farsed: stuffed
faste: near by
fayn: gladly
fee simple: freehold
felawe: companion, also a rascal
felawshipe: company, fellowship
felicitee: happiness
fer: far
ferme: annual payment
ferne: distant
ferre: further
ferrer: further
ferreste: furthest
ferther: further
ferthing: a fourth part, a spot, a farthing
festne: fasten
fetis: neat
fetisly: neatly, accurately, properly
fetys: well made

feyne: make up
feyned: imitation
fil: fell
fille: fell
finch: finch (a bird)
Finistere: Galicia in Spain
fissh: fish
fithele: fiddle
flaterye: flattery, lies
Flaundres: Flanders
Flaundrish: in the style of Flanders
flex: flax
flok: flock
flour: flower
flour-de-lys: lily
floytinge: playing the flute, or whistling
foo: foe
foot-mantel: outer skirt used when riding
for-pyned: wasted away
foreward: agreement
forheed: forehead
forme: propriety
forneys: furnace
forster: forester
fortunen: foretell
forward: agreement
fother: cart-load
foughten: fought
fowel: bird
fowles: birds
frankeleyn: prosperous landowner
fraternitee: brotherhood, fraternity, guild
fredom: integrity
freend: friend

freendes: friends
Frensh: French
fro: from
fustian: thick cotton cloth
fyn: fine
fyne: fine
fyneste: most expensive, best
fyr-reed: fiery red
fyve: five

gadrede: gathered
Galice: Galicia: the district containing the shrine of St James at Compostella
galyngale: sweet cyperus root
gamed: pleasant
garleek: garlic
gat-toothed: gap-toothed (see textual note)
gauded: furnished with large beads
Gaunt: Ghent
gay: showily dressed
geere: utensils
gelding: gelding, a neutered or castrated horse
gentil: excellent, well born
gerland: garland
Gernade: Granada
gerner: garner, grain store, granary
ginglen: gingle
gipoun: tight-fitting vest, doublet
gipser: pouch
girdle(es): belt(s)
girles: young people of either sex
girt: gathered together
glaringe: glaring

glas: glass, mirror
y-go: given over to
gobet: small portion
goliardeys: teller of bawdy jokes
good: properly
goon: go
goost: ghost, spirit
goot: goat
Gootland: Gotland in the Baltic
goune: gown
governaunce: management
governynge: control
grace: favour
graunt: grant
grece: grease
Grete See: the Mediterranean
gretter: larger
greyn: corn
grope: test, sound out
ground: texture
grounded: trained, educated
grys: expensive grey fur
gyde: guide, leader
gynglen: jingling
gyse: fashion, way

Haberdassher: a seller of materials
  or hats
habergeoun: coat of mail
halfe: half
halle: dining hall
halwes: shrines
happe: circumstance
hardily: certainly
hardy: brave, rash, sturdy
harlot: low-living person
harlotryes: scurrilous things
harneised: equipped

haunt: skill
havenes: places to anchor
heed: head
heeld: look after
heeng: hung
heer: hair
heeth: natural open space,
  heath
heigh: high
hem: them
heng: hung
hente (l. 700): called
hente (l. 301): obtain
herberwe: inn (literally harbour)
herde: cow-herd, shepherd
heres: hairs
hethen: heathen
hethenesse: heathen lands
heve of harre: heave off its
  hinges
hevene: heaven
hewe: colour, complexion
highte: called
him-selven: himself
hipes: hips
hir: their
hire: fee
holpen: helped
holt: wood, grove
holwe: hollow
holy: holy
hond: wrist
hoolly: wholly
Hooste: Host
hoot: hot
hoote: hot
hors: horse or horses
hosen: stockings

hostelrye: inn, public house
hostiler: publican
hote: hotly
houres: astronomical hours (see textual note)
householdere: head of household
humour: humour (see textual note)
hy sentence: learning expressed in maxims
hyer: upper
hyndreste: hindmost
hyne: farm labourer

ilke: same
in good poynt: handsome
infect: invalid
inspired: breathed upon, quickened

Ianglere: loud talker
Iapes: tricks
Iay: jay (a bird)
jet: fashion, style
Iolitee: greater comfort, display
Iuge: adjudicate
juggement: ruling
Iuste: joust

kan: knew how
keep: care
kene: sharp
kepe: take care
keper: head, prior
kept: guarded
knarre: fellow
knight of the shire: Member of Parliament

knobbes: boils, lumps
y-knowe: known
koude: knew how

laas: cord, lace
y-lad: carried
lakkede: lacked
large: freely
late: recently, just
latoun: pinchbeck, base metal
Latyn: Latin
lazar: leper
leed: cauldron
leet: let
lekes: leeks
lene: lend
lengthe: height
lerned: learned
lessoun: lesson
lest: delight, pleasure
leste: if you please
Lettow: Lithuania
letuaries: electuaries, medicines
lever: prefer
lewed: unlearned, not in holy orders
leyd: laid in
licentiat: licensed to hear confession
licour: moisture
limitour: one who begs within an assigned district
list: pleased
liste: pleased
listes: place where tournaments were held
litarge: white lead
litel: little

liveree: livery, uniforms
lodemenage: piloting
logik: philosophy
lokkes: locks of hair
lond, of a: country, in the
londes: lands, countries
looth: loath
Lordyngs: my Lords
lore: law
lough: low
love-dayes: days fixed for settling disputes
love-knotte: a complicated twist of loops suggesting endless love
lowly: humble
luce: pike (a fish)
lust: delight
lusty: happy, vigorous
lyed: lied
Lyeys: located in Armenia
lyk: like
y-lyk: like
lyned: lined
lyte: least rich, important
lyve: live
lyven: live

maad: made
magik: magic, skills (see textual note)
maister: high-placed churchman
maistres: masters
maistry: superiority, position of responsibility
make: draught
maladye: sickness
male: bag
maner: sort of, type

manere: bearing
mantel: train
marchant: merchant
marshal: major-domo, chief steward
martir: martyr
mary-bones: marrow bones
Maudelayne: after St Mary Magdalene
Maunciple: buyer of provisions for college or Inn of Court
Maure: Maurus (see textual note)
mayde: virgin
mede: field
medlee: coat of mixed rich stuff or colour
mercenarie: hireling
mere: mare
merye: happy, jolly
meschief: bad times
mesurable: moderate
mete: food, meal times, meat
mewe: coop for fattening birds
Millere: miller
miscarie: come to harm
mister: skilled trade
moiste: moist
mone: moon
moot: must, should
mormal: an open sore
morne: morning
mortal: fatal
mortreux: thick meat or fish soup
morwe: morning
morwe-song: matins, i.e. what is agreed for today
mottlee: a coat of mixed rich stuff or colours

mous: mouse
muche: great, rich, important
muchel: greatly
murierly: merrily
mury: merry
myrie: merry
myrthe: happiness
myselven: myself

namore: no more
narette: do not call it
narwe: narrow
nas: was not
nat: not
natheles: nevertheless
nedeth: needs
neet: cattle
nightertale: night-time
nones: occasion
Nonne: Nun
noon: none
noot: know not
norissyng: nourishing
Northfolk: Norfolk
nose-thirles: nostrils
not-heed: closely cropped hair
  (see textual note)
nought: not
nouthe: now, at this time
nowthe: now
ny: close
nyce: delicate

o: one
o-wher: anywhere
obstinat: stubborn
offring: offerings from
  parishioners made voluntarily

offyce: secular employment
ofte: many
oille of tartre: cream of tartar
oistre: oyster
oon: one
ooth: oath
oother: other
othes: oaths
ounces: in small portions
oure lady: Virgin Mary
out-rydere: one who looks after
  outlying granges etc.
outrely: outright
overeste courtepy: outer short
  cloak
overlippe: upper lip
overspradde: spread out
owne: own
oynement: ointment
oynons: onions

pace (l. 36): go on
pace (l. 175): pass by
pacient: patient
Palatye: in Anatolia
palfrey: riding horse
palmers: pilgrims to the Holy
  Land
pardee: by God, indeed
Pardoner: seller of pardons (see
  textual note)
pardouns: pardons (see textual
  note)
parfit: perfect, i.e. complete
parfyt: perfect
parisshe: parish
parisshens: parishioners
partrich: partridge

parvys: portico of St Paul's or Westminster Abbey, or a students' mock trial

pas: walking pace

patente: letters from the King appointing a Judge

pecok arwes: arrows with peacock's feathers used as flights

pees: peace

peire: a set

penaunce: penance

peple: people

per-chaunce: perhaps

perced: pierced

pers: bluish grey

persoun: parson

pestilence: plague

peyned: took pains, endeavoured

phisik: medicine

phisyk: medicine

Picardye: Picardy

pigges: pigs

pilwe-beer: pillow case

pin: brooch

pinche: find fault with

pinched: pleated

pitaunce: a gift of food

pitous: full of pity

plenteous: plenteous

plesaunt: kindly, pleasantly behaved

plesen: please

pleyen: relax

pleyn: pure

pleyn by rote: recite by heart

pleyn commissioun: personal letter of appointment as Judge

point: physical condition

pomely: dappled

poraille: a contemptuous word for poor people

port: bearing

post: inn, posting house

pouches: purses

poudre-marchant: sharp flavouring powder

povre: poor

poynaunt: spicy

poynt: nub of the matter

praktisour: practitioner

preche: preach

preest: priest

prelat: man of the Church

presse: curling tongs, mould

y-preved: proved

prikasour: hard rider or a tracker of hares

priketh: excites

prikyng: hard riding or tracking hares

pris: price

prively: secretly

propre: own

proprely: faithfully

Pruce: Prussia

prys: prize, price

pulle: pluck, i.e. cheat

pulled: plucked

pultrye: poultry

y-punishhed: punished

purchas: profits from begging

purchasour: buyer of land

purfiled: edged with fur

purs: purse

purtreye: draw

pylled: thin haired

pynnes: pins

quik: pithy
quik-silver: mercury
quyte yow mede: duly reward you

rage: indulge in dalliance
Ram: the astrological sign of Aries
raughte: reach out
rebel: rebellious, in disagreement
recchelees: careless, disregarding rules
reckenings: bills
reckenynges: bills
recorde: recall it to your memory
rede: red
reed (l. 667): adviser
reed (l. 461): red
Reeve: estate manager
reherce: repeat
rekening: account
rekne: calculate
relikes: relics
remenaunt: remainder
renning: running
rente: income
reportour: umpire, judge
resons: opinions
resoun: reason, reasonable, agree
reule: discipline, rules
reuled: governed
reverence: modest, respect
reyn: rain
reysed: made a military expedition
y-ronne: run
rood: rode
roos: rose
roost: roast meat
rote (l. 236): fiddle
rote (l.2, 425): root

Rouncival: Roncesvalles (see textual note)
rouncy: common hackney horse
royalliche: like a queen
Ruce: Russia
rudeliche: coarsely

sangwyn: blood red, confident
Satalye: on the south coast of Asia Minor
sauce: sauce or soup
saugh: saw
sautrye: psaltery, a musical instrument
savith: save
sawcefleem: afflicted with pimples
sawe: saw
scalled: scabby
scarsly: economically
scathe: shame, pity
science: knowledge, skills
sclendre: slender
scole: manner, school of
scoler: scholar
scoleye: attend university or study
seche: look for
see: sea
sege: siege
seigh: saw
Seint Iulian: St Julian, patron saint of hospitality
Seint-Jame: St James
Seinte Loy: St Eligius see textual note)
seke: ill, sickly, seek out, visit
seken: seek
semely: becoming, proper
semi-cope: short cloak

sendal: rich, thin silk
sentence: instruction, learning
sergeant of the lawe: senior barrister
servaunts: servants
servisable: willing to serve
sessiouns: meeting of Justices of the Peace
sethe: seethe, boil
seyl: sail
shadwed: shaded
y-shadwed: overshadowed
shamefastnesse: modesty, shyness
shapen yow: intend
shaply: fitted
sheef: sheaf
sheeldes: crowns (coins)
shene: shining
shine: shin
shire: county
shirreve: sheriff
shiten: dung covered, dirtied
sho: shoe
shoon: shone
y-shorn: cut
short-sholdered: thick set
short: little, small
shorte: shorten
shoures: showers
y-shryve: confessed
shuldres: shoulders
sikerly: certainly
sin: since
singinge: singing
sire: president, chairman
slee: slay
sleighte: trick
smerte: unpleasant

smoot: smote
smyling: smiling
snewed: snowed
snibben: scold, rebuke
solas: amusement
solempne: festive, solemn
solempnely: pompously
som-del: somewhat, rather
somer: summer
Som(o)nour: man who summoned people to ecclesiastical courts (see textual note)
sondry: various
sonne: sun
soong: sang
soothly: truly
sop: piece of cake or bread
soper: supper
sort: destiny
sote: sweet
soun: sound
souninge: concerning, proclaiming
souple: soft and close-fitting
sovereyn: highest
sowe: sow, pig
sowne: sound
space: period of time
spak: spoke
spanne: span, hand's breadth
sparwe: sparrow
spores: spurs
springe: spring, rise
spyced: scrupulous
staf: staff, stick
statut: statute
stemed: shone
stepe: bright, fiery
sterres: stars

stewe: fish pond
stif: strong bass voice
stiwardes: stewards
stonde: be ranked
stonden: stand
stoor: store
stot: cob
straunge: foreign, unknown
streem: stream or river
streit: strict
strem: stream or river
stremes: currents
strondes: shores
stryke: hank
substaunce: money
subtilly: cleverly
suffisaunce: contentment
suffre: allow
superfluitee: excessive
surcote: long overcoat
swerd: sword
swere: swear
swich: such
swink: work
swinken: labour
swinkere: worker
swyn: pigs
symple: unaffected
sythes: times

tabard: herald's coat, ploughman's loose smock or sleeveless jacket
taille: on credit
take: keep
takel: equipment
talen: to tell tales
Tapicer: upholsterer

tappestere: female publican
targe: shield
tart: sharp
tarynge: tarrying, delay
y-taught: taught
telleth: tells
temple: Inn of Court
tendre: tender, new
termes: express in proper form
text: frequently quoted statement
y-teyd: tied
than: then
ther-to: in addition
there as: where that
thereof: of this
thereto: moreover
thestat: the social position
thikke: muscular
thing: legal agreement
thombe: thumb
thresshe: thresh
thries: three times
thriftily: serviceably
thryse: three times
thynne: thin
tipet: loose hood
toft: tuft
togidre: together
tollen: take payment or toll
Tramissene: in western Algeria
tretys: long and well-shaped
trewe: true, honest
trompe: trumpet, trumpeter
trouthe: integrity
trowe: believe
trussed: folded up in
tukked: tucked up round him
Turkye: Turkey

tweye: two
twynne: depart
tydes: tides

undergrowe: short
undertake: take responsibility
untrewe: false
usage: skills

vavasour: sub-vassal (see textual note)
venerie: hunting
verdit: decision, opinion
vernicle: a miniature of the face of Christ (see textual note)
verrail: very
verray: truly
vertu: vital energy
veyl: veil
veyne: channel for sap
viage: journey
vigilyes: celebrations
vileinye: unbecoming in a gentleman
visage: face
vitaille: victuals, food
vouche-sauf: promise, agree
voys: voice

wandrynge: wandering
wantown: wild, lively, loose living
wantownesse: affectation
war: aware, let him know of, wary
wastel-breed: bread made of the best flour
waterlees: out of water
wateryng: watering place for horses

wayted: looked for
Webbe: male weaver
wel: well
wende: go (as in he 'wends' his way)
wente: walked
weren: were
werken: make happen, do
werre: war, service
werte: wart
wex: wax
weye: wayside
weyeden: weighed
whan: when
wheither: whether
whelkes: pimples
whelpe: like a puppy
whoso: whomsoever
whyl: while
whylom: once upon a time
whyt: white
whyte: white
widwe: widow
wif: wife
wight: person
wimpel: a covering for a nun's neck and head
y-wimpled: covered with wimples
winne: prove him in arrears
winnyng: profits
wiste: knew
wit: intelligence
with alle: moreover
withholde: kept in retirement
withouten: without
withseye: disagree with, contradict
wo: in trouble

wodecraft: woodcraft, forestry
wolden: wished
wonderly: wonderfully
wone: custom
woning(e): house, dwelling place
wood: mad
woot: know
worstede: woven cloth
worthy: honourable
wrastling: wrestling
wrighte: craftsman
y-wroght: made
wroghte: did good deeds
wrooth: angry
wrought: made
wryte: write
wyd: wide
wyde: large
wyn: wine
wynd: wind
wynne: win
wys: deliberation, matter for discussion, prudent, wise, learned

y-bore: carried
y-chapped: capped
y-come: come (past participle)
y-drawe: stolen
y-falle: fallen
y-go: given over to
y-knowe: known

y-lad: carried
y-lyk: like
y-preved: proved
y-punishhed: punished
y-ronne: run
y-shadwed: overshadowed
y-shorn: cut
y-shryve: confessed
y-taught: taught
y-teyd: tied
y-wimpled: covered with wimples, i.e. cloths; wearing many veils over her neck and head
y-wroght: made
yaf: gave
yë: eye
yeddinges: popular songs
yeeve: utensils
yeldhalle: guildhall
yelding: yield
yeldynge: yield
yeman: yeoman, senior servant
yemanly: as befits a yeoman
yerde: rod, three foot measure
yeve: give
yeven: gave
yit: yet
yive: give
ymages: astrological signs or talismans
yow: you

Zephirus: personification of the West wind

Examination Questions

Read the following passage, and answer all the questions printed beneath it:

With us ther was a DOCTOUR OF PHISYK,
In al this world ne was ther noon him lyk
To speke of phisik and of surgerye;
For he was grounded in astronomye.
He kepte his pacient a ful greet del   5
In houres, by his magik naturel.
Wel coude he fortunen the ascendent
Of his images for his pacient.
He knew the cause of everich maladye,
Were it of hoot or cold, or moiste, or drye,   10
And where engendred, and of what humour;
He was a verrey parfit *practisour*.
The cause y-knowe, and of his harm the *rote*,
Anon he yaf the seke man his *bote*.
Ful redy hadde he his *apothecaries*,   15
To sende him *drogges* and his *letuaries*,
For ech of hem made other for to winne;
Hir frendschipe nas nat newe to biginne.
Wel knew he the olde Esculapius,
And Deiscorides, and eek Rufus,   20
Old Ypocras, Haly, and Galien;
Serapion, Razis, and Avicen;
Averrois, Damascien, and Constantyn;
Bernard, and Gatesden, and Gilbertyn.
Of his diete mesurable was he,   25
For it was of no superfluitee,

But of greet norissing and digestible.
His studie was but litel on the Bible.
In sangwin and in pers he clad was al,   30
Lyned with tafeta and with sendal;
And yet he was but esy of dispence;
He kepte that he wan in pestilence.
For gold in phisik is a cordial
Therefore he lovede gold in special.

(i)   Briefly explain *humour* (line 11).   [2]
(ii) Turn into clear modern English lines 12–16 (*He was ...
      letuaries*). Take care to bring out the meaning of the six italicized
      words.   [8]
(iii) What impressions do you get of the Doctor's character and
      attitudes from this extract?   [10]

                                        Oxford Local Examinations, 1980

Read the following passage, and answer **all** the questions printed
beneath it:

A good man was ther of religioun,
And was a povre PERSOUN of a toun;
But riche he was of holy thoght and werk.
He was also a lerned man, a clerk,
That Cristes gospel trewely wolde preche;   5
His parisshens devoutly wolde he teche.
Benigne he was, and wonder diligent,
And in adversitee ful pacient;
And swich he was y-preved ofte sythes.
Ful looth were him to cursen for his tythes,   10
But rather wolde he yeven, out of doute,
Un-to his povre parisshens aboute
Of his offring, and eek of his substaunce.
He coude in litel thing han suffisaunce.
Wyd was his parisshe, and houses fer a-sonder,   15
But he ne lafte nat, for reyn ne thonder,
In siknes nor in *meschief*, to visyte
The *ferreste* in his parisshe, muche and *lyte*,

Up-on his feet, and in his hand a staf.
This noble *ensample* to his *sheep* he yaf,   20
That first he *wroghte*, and afterward he taughte;
Out of the gospel he tho wordes caughte;
And this figure he added eek ther-to,
That if gold ruste, what shal iren do?
For if a preest be foul, on whom we truste,   25
No wonder is a lewed man to ruste;

(i) Explain *cursen for his tythes* (line 10).   [2]

(ii) Turn into clear modern English lines 15–21 (*Wyd was . . . taughte*).
Take care to bring out the meaning of the six italicized words.
[8]

(iii) In what ways does the Parson compare favourably with any **two**
of the following: the Friar; the Pardoner; the Prioress; the Monk?
[10]

Either, (*a*) 'Some women were surprisingly independent in Chaucer's
day.' Discuss, with reference to the Prioress and the Wife of Bath.
[20]

Or, (*b*) Show how Chaucer describes people's appearances in order
to bring out their characters. Refer to **two or three** of the pilgrims,
excluding the Doctor of Physic.   [20]

Oxford Local Examinations, 1980

Read the following passage, and answer the questions printed beneath
it:

A KNIGHT ther was, and that a worthy man,
That fro the tyme that he first bigan
To ryden out, he loved chivalrye,
Trouthe and honour, fredom and curteisye.
Ful worthy was he in his lordes werre,   5
And therto hadde he riden (no man ferre)
As wel in Cristendom as hethenesse,
And ever honoured for his worthinesse.

At Alisaundre he was, whan it was wonne;
Ful ofte tyme he hadde the bord bigonne   10
Aboven alle naciouns in Pruce.
In Lettow hadde he reysed and in Ruce,
No Cristen man so ofte of his degree.
In Gernade at the sege eek hadde he be
Of Algezir, and riden in Belmarye.   15
At Lyeys was he, and at Satalye,
Whan they were wonne; and in the Grete See
At many a noble aryve hadde he be.
At mortal batailles hadde he been fiftene,
And foughten for our feith at Tramissene   20
In listes thryes, and ay slayn his foo.
This ilke worthy knight had been also
Somtyme with the lord of Palatye,
Ageyn another hethen in Turkye:
And evermore he hadde a sovereyn prys.   25
And though that he were worthy, he was wys,
And of his port as meke as is a mayde.
He never yet no vileinye ne sayde
In al his lyf, un-to no maner wight.
He was a verray parfit gentil knight.   30

(i) Turn into clear modern English lines 5–8 (*Ful worthy was he
    ... for his worthinesse*), and lines 26–29 (*And though ... maner
    wight*).   [10]

(ii) How does Chaucer in this passage build up an impression of the
     Knight as *a worthy man* (line 1)?   [10]

Choose **three** of the following pilgrims, and show how Chaucer's
description of their outward appearance reflects their personalities:
the Squire; the Prioress; the Wife of Bath; the Pardoner; the Franklin;
the Reeve; the Clerk.   [20]

Oxford Local Examinations, 1977

Read the following passages carefully, then answer the questions printed beneath them.

A

His resons he spak ful solempnely,
Souninge alway th'encrees of his winning.
He wolde the see were kept for any thing
Bitwixe Middelburgh and Orewelle.
Wel coude he in eschaunge sheeldes selle.   5
This worthy man ful wel his wit bisette:
Ther wiste no wight that he was in dette,
So estatly was he of his governaunce
With his bargaynes and his chevissaunce.

  (i) Who is described in this passage?

 (ii) Give the meanings of *souninge* (line 2), *chevissaunce* (line 9).   [2]

(iii) Explain fully the significance of line 5. (You are **not** required to translate it.)   [3]

(iv) How completely does this passage condemn the character it describes?   [4]

B

Wel wiste he, by the droghte, and by the reyn,
The yelding of his seed, and of his greyn.
His lordes sheep, his neet, his dayerye,
His swyn, his hors, his stoor, and his pultrye,
Was hoolly in this reves governing,
And by his covenaunt yaf the rekening,
Sin that his lord was twenty yeer of age;
Ther coude no man bringe him in arrerage.
Ther nas bailliff, ne herde, ne other hyne,
That he ne knew his sleighte and his covyne;
They were adrad of him, as of the deeth.
His woning was ful fair up-on an heeth,
With grene treës shadwed was his place.
He coude bettre than his lord purchace.

Ful riche he was astored prively,
His lord wel coude he plesen subtilly,
To yeve and lene him of his owne good,
And have a thank, and yet a cote and hood.

(i) Give the meaning of *neet* (line 3), *hyne* (line 9), *covyne* (line 10), *wonyng* (line 12).   [4]

(ii) Rewrite in clear modern English lines 15–18: *Ful riche ... cote and hood.*   [8]

(iii) Give a brief account of the character of the Reeve as seen in this passage.   [8]

1. Discuss the attitude to the Church you find in *The Prologue*.   [30]

2. What is the impression you have received from *The Prologue* of the commercial and professional classes in Chaucer's time?   [30]

Oxford and Cambridge Schools Examination Board, 1972

MORE ABOUT PENGUINS, PELICANS AND PUFFINS

For further information about books available from Penguins please write to Dept EP, Penguin Books Ltd, Harmondsworth, Middlesex UB7 0DA.

In the U.S.A.: For a complete list of books available from Penguins in the United States write to Dept DG, Penguin Books, 299 Murray Hill Parkway, East Rutherford, New Jersey 07073.

In Canada: For a complete list of books available from Penguins in Canada write to Penguin Books Canada Ltd, 2801 John Street, Markham, Ontario L3R 1B4.

In Australia: For a complete list of books available from Penguins in Australia write to the Marketing Department, Penguin Books Australia Ltd, P.O. Box 257, Ringwood, Victoria 3134.

In New Zealand: For a complete list of books available from Penguins in New Zealand write to the Marketing Department, Penguin Books (N.Z.) Ltd, Private Bag, Takapuna, Auckland 9.

In India: For a complete list of books available from Penguins in India write to Penguin Overseas Ltd, 706 Eros Apartments, 56 Nehru Place, New Delhi 110019.

Penguin Passnotes

Carefully tailored to the requirements of the main examination boards (for O-level or CSE exams), Penguin Passnotes are an invaluable companion to your studies.

Covering a wide range of English literature texts as well as many other subjects, Penguin Passnotes will include:

English Literature

A Man for All Seasons
Chaucer: General Prologue
Cider With Rosie
Great Expectations
Jane Eyre
Pride and Prejudice

Silas Marner
The Mayor of Casterbridge
The Woman in White
To Kill a Mockingbird
Wuthering Heights

Shakespeare

As You Like It
Henry IV, Part I
Julius Caesar
Macbeth

The Merchant of Venice
Twelfth Night
Romeo and Julet

Subject Areas

Biology
Chemistry
Economics
English Language
French
Geography

Modern World History
Physics
Human Biology
Mathematics
Modern Mathematics

Plus fully annotated editions of your set texts in The Pelican Shakespeare

PENGUIN OMNIBUSES

☐ **The Penguin Complete Sherlock Holmes**
Sir Arthur Conan Doyle £5.50

With all fifty-six classic short stories, plus *A Study in Scarlet, The Sign of Four, The Hound of the Baskervilles* and *The Valley of Fear*, this volume contains the remarkable career of Baker Street's most famous resident.

☐ **The Alexander Trilogy Mary Renault** £4.95

Containing *Fire from Heaven, The Persian Boy* and *Funeral Games* – her re-creation of Ancient Greece acclaimed by Gore Vidal as 'one of this century's most unexpectedly original works of art'.

☐ **The Penguin Complete Novels of George Orwell** £5.50

Containing the six novels: *Animal Farm, Burmese Days, A Clergyman's Daughter, Coming Up For Air, Keep the Aspidistra Flying* and *Nineteen Eighty-Four.*

☐ **The Penguin Essays of George Orwell** £4.95

Famous pieces on 'The Decline of the English Murder', 'Shooting an Elephant', political issues and P. G. Wodehouse feature in this edition of forty-one essays, criticism and sketches – all classics of English prose.

☐ **The Penguin Collected Stories of**
Isaac Bashevis Singer £4.95

Forty-seven marvellous tales of Jewish magic, faith and exile. 'Never was the Nobel Prize more deserved . . . He belongs with the giants' – *Sunday Times*

☐ **Famous Trials Harry Hodge and James H. Hodge** £3.50

From Madeleine Smith to Dr Crippen and Lord Haw-Haw, this volume contains the most sensational murder and treason trials, selected by John Mortimer from the classic Penguin Famous Trials series.

PENGUIN OMNIBUSES

☐ *The Penguin Complete Novels of Jane Austen* £5.95

Containing the seven great novels: *Sense and Sensibility*, *Pride and Prejudice*, *Mansfield Park*, *Emma*, *Northanger Abbey*, *Persuasion* and *Lady Susan*.

☐ *The Penguin Kenneth Grahame* £3.95

Containing his wonderful evocations of childhood – *The Golden Age* and *Dream Days* – plus his masterpiece, *The Wind in the Willows*, originally written for his son and since then loved by readers of all ages.

☐ *The Titus Books* **Mervyn Peake** £5.95

Titus Groan, *Gormenghast* and *Titus Alone* form this century's masterpiece of Gothic fantasy. 'It is uniquely brilliant . . . a rich wine of fancy' – Anthony Burgess

☐ *Life at Thrush Green* **'Miss Read'** £3.50

Full of gossip, humour and charm, these three novels – *Thrush Green*, *Winter in Thrush Green* and *News from Thrush Green* – make up a delightful picture of life in a country village.

☐ *The Penguin Classic Crime Omnibus* £3.95

Julian Symons's original anthology includes all the masters – Doyle, Poe, Highsmith, Graham Greene and P. D. James – represented by some of their less familiar but most surprising and ingenious crime stories.

☐ *The Penguin Great Novels of D. H. Lawrence* £4.95

Containing *Sons and Lovers*, *The Rainbow* and *Women in Love*: the three famous novels in which Lawrence brought his story of human nature, love and sexuality to its fullest flowering.

PENGUIN OMNIBUSES

☐ **The Penguin Brontë Sisters**   £4.95

Containing Anne Brontë's *The Tenant of Wildfell Hall*, Charlotte Brontë's *Jane Eyre* and Emily Brontë's *Wuthering Heights*.

☐ **The Penguin Thomas Hardy 1**   £4.95

His four early Wessex novels: *Under the Greenwood Tree, Far From the Madding Crowd, The Return of the Native* and *The Mayor of Casterbridge*.

☐ **The Penguin Thomas Hardy 2**   £5.50

Containing the four later masterpieces: *The Trumpet-Major, The Woodlanders, Tess of the D'Urbervilles* and *Jude the Obscure*.

These books should be available at all good bookshops or news-agents, but if you live in the UK or the Republic of Ireland and have difficulty in getting to a bookshop, they can be ordered by post Please indicate the titles required and fill in the form below.

NAME _____ BLOCK CAPITALS

ADDRESS _____

_____

_____

Enclose a cheque or postal order payable to The Penguin Bookshop to cover the total price of books ordered, plus 50p for postage. Readers in the Republic of Ireland should send £IR equivalent to the sterling prices, plus 67p for postage. Send to: The Penguin Bookshop, 54/56 Bridlesmith Gate, Nottingham, NG1 2GP.

You can also order by phoning (0602) 599295, and quoting your Barclaycard or Access number.

Every effort is made to ensure the accuracy of the price and availability of books at the time of going to press, but it is sometimes necessary to increase prices and in these circumstances retail prices may be shown on the covers of books which may differ from the prices shown in this list or elsewhere. This list is not an offer to supply any book.

This order service is only available to residents in the UK and the Republic of Ireland.